Host for the Most

A handbook for getting the most out of your home-share rental —

written by an obsessive-compulsive, but experienced host

Donna Evans-Deyermond

Turn "lookers" into "bookers"--entice prospective guests with a vision of what life is like at your vacation rental home.

Host for the Most
By Donna Evans-Deyermond

Copyright 2019 by Donna Evans-Deyermond
Cover Copyright 2019 by Donna Evans-Deyermond
Cover Design by Ginny Glass

ISBN-13: 978-0-57845-024-7

Also available in ebook format.

Published by Donna L. Evans Public Relations
donnaevansdeyermond.com

Printed in the United States of America.

Contents

Introduction

Are you looking at that seldom-used spare room and thinking it might help bring in some extra cash? Or thinking your vacation home could start paying its own way if you rented it out on a home-sharing web site? Or maybe you live in an area of the country where the cost of housing is out-of-sight and you need to rent part of your home to make the mortgage payments. You are right on track—both vacationers and businesspeople are using rentals by owners more and more. Both are looking for the comfort and convenience of a "home away from home" when they travel, rather than a cold hotel room where they can barely get a good cup of coffee in the morning.

Becoming a host and sharing your primary or vacation home sounds like a great idea, and it is a great idea. However, if you want to be successful, short-term rentals are like everything else—you get back what you put in. My husband and I have been using home-sharing sites to find accommodations for more than 14 years, and we've rented out three different homes over the past 12 years. From taking photos to describing your listing, to answering inquiries, to equipping your place, to checking people in and getting the place cleaned between checking-out and checking-in guests—sharing your home is fun, but it's not "easy" money. If you take it one step at a time, however, you will get it done, make some cash, and great new friends along the way.

Before we get started and you begin to think this book is about an elitist couple who can afford such things as a vacation home and traveling the world, let me say a bit about us. My husband, Cal, was a school administrator who worked for 42 years before he retired—albeit with a nice pension. I was employed in a PR position until he retired in 2004, and I still work part-time. Cal used his retirement savings to build the house we owned in Mexico, and along the way we've put a lot of sweat equity into the homes we've owned (and we continue to do so).

I understand what it means to do all the scraping and painting, replace broken toilet parts and door knobs, stain decks and scrub terraces—because that's what we have done—and continue to do to this day. To rent our home-share units, I took the photos, wrote the descriptions, set up the web pages, handled all the bookings, laundered sheets and towels, sewed curtains and made sure the places got cleaned between guests and during their stays.

Cal collected rental fees, returned damage deposits, was the major "Mr. Fix-it," got estimates for the things we couldn't do ourselves and balanced the books at the end of the month. Like I said, not "easy money"—but worthwhile all the same. We both enjoy looking after our homes, but most of all, we enjoy people and discovered home-sharing to be very fulfilling. The renters we met along the way taught us patience, how to show grace under pressure and overall, have greatly enriched our lives.

We owned a house in Sayulita, Mexico, with a casita (a studio apartment) that we started renting from the day construction was completed in December of 2006, when we moved into the upstairs unit (the main house) to spend our first winter in paradise. Our idea was to live in the house from January to May, rent it as much as possible from June to December; and rent the casita year-round to help meet expenses. We knew when we built the house there would be monthly upkeep, whether we were living there or not.

Tropical climates are hard on houses, which means lots of power-washing masonry, tile floors and outdoor furniture, refinishing wood, and replacing appliances, plus we had to pay someone to manage it when we weren't there. We also rented a house we owned and lived in close to a ski area outside of our home base, Buffalo, N.Y.

On the other side of the coin, we started out as renters in Sayulita and San Miguel, Mexico. (It was on this trip that we found our lot in Sayulita and decided to build our vacation home there.) We discovered then that home-sharing was a great way to vacation and get to know the locals, so every big trip we've taken since has involved either a rental or a house-swap. We've traveled all over the United Kingdom, seen Paris and Marseilles, been to Barcelona and the beaches down the coast of Spain, and most recently, visited seven cities in the north of Italy. We haven't ignored the U.S.—we've been to Palm Springs, the outer banks of North Carolina, the Adirondacks in New York, and the Portage and Erie Lakes in Ohio.

Along the way we've had some experiences that have been frustrating at the time, but in the rearview mirror have given us a lot of laughs. There was the host of the place in France, for example, who told us the chateau in which her condo was located was an easy walk from the train station. She neglected to mention that was only if you were willing to drag your suitcase through the freshly plowed fields, not by road.

Then there was the tiny half-bath located on the balcony of the house in San Miguel. There, if you had to sit down, the only way to pull your pants up was to open the door, stand and turn so your bare behind was facing out the door (yes, it's a balcony, open to the street). Only after mooning the street could you bend over to get the pants from around your knees back up to your waist. And then there was our host in Mexico City, who was a dead-ringer for Shrek—except in complexion, of course!

What I'm saying is, I feel qualified to share what I've learned about hosting from both perspectives—hosting and renting. I also happen to be pretty particular, so I notice when things are not great, and I have particular friends who also rent from home-sharing sites who have contributed their pet peeves. What's the most frequent one? Not enough wine glasses. It seems simple, but it's pretty frustrating when two couples show up to a two-bedroom rental and there's one, lonely wine glass in the cupboard. What tastes better at the end of a long day of travel than a nice glass (and I mean "nice glass") of the wine you just picked up at the local grocery store? (Well … some folks might prefer a beer!)

While real estate might depend on location, location, location; home sharing depends on reviews, reviews, reviews. That's the rule with pretty much everything you want to sell these days, and you are selling your place when you rent it out. The better your reviews, the more you'll rent; the more you rent, the more money you'll make. Good reviews also mean you can charge more for your place, which in turn means more cash in your pocket. Our house in Mexico more than paid for itself, even with our living there four months out of the year during the high rental season. It also provided us with mad money to use to travel other parts of the world.

Of course you can't please all of the people all of the time. We've had our share of challenges and even some bad reviews—but I'm hoping this book will help readers avoid many of the pitfalls. I know one thing for sure—you'll always have enough wine glasses, right?

Chapter 1

Creating Your Listing—From Nuts and Bolts to the Sales Pitch

When you join the home-sharing rental business, you will find there are experts available who can help you with everything—taking photos and videos, setting up your web page, managing your rentals and managing your house. All of these services come with a price. There are some things you won't be able to do yourself, such as check people in or clean and do laundry between guests if you aren't in the same town. Those will definitely go down in the "expense" column of your ledger. If you want to come out in the black at the bottom of that ledger, it's to your advantage to do as much as you can yourself.

Anecdote: When we first started renting we paid a lovely couple 15 percent of every booking to manage the rentals and check people in. We had met this couple, who worked under the umbrella of a real estate agency, when we first were renters in Sayulita and were considering buying a place there. They were very personable, efficient and well-regarded in the community, since they handled bookings for probably around 100 houses.

When we started out, our home wasn't established—we didn't have a rental history or those ever-so-important glowing reviews—so we weren't getting many renters. It didn't take long to realize handling bookings isn't that challenging and we were already paying a house manager who was quite capable of doing the check-ins.

We said adios to the charming couple, staying on good terms because we promised to send them referrals whenever possible (never burn any bridges in a small town) and I started handling bookings. This gave me the opportunity to "sell" the house to people who were considering other places, which was something the management agency wasn't doing. They handled houses for so many other owners, and got paid no matter which house they rented, so it didn't matter to them if they booked our house or someone else's. I, on the other hand, had a vested interest in developing a rapport with prospects and that rapport frequently resulted in a booking. There was also less back and forth for renters because if they had questions, I could answer directly. Plus, they could negotiate directly if they wanted to get a deal on the fees.

Before long our bookings increased, we began to collect reviews and, not only were we making more money, it was in our pockets sooner because we had eliminated one of the middlemen (the home-sharing sites are still in the middle). If you are sharing your home to make a profit, you'll want to do as much of the work involved as possible. You have to decide what you're capable of handling and what you need to farm out. That said, let's begin at the beginning.

Building a "Suck 'Em In!" Web Page

Each booking web site has a different site map and some are more user-friendly than others. Set aside several hours to do this project because I guarantee you'll be frustrated at some point in the process. When that happens, step away from the computer (to prevent throwing it out the window) and go have a glass of whatever beverage calms you down.

To begin, I recommend writing your description and headline in a word program, then copying and pasting to the various sites you decide to use.

Obviously, the headline should be eye-catching and short, so start by thinking "sensational." Look at some of the headlines in the *New York Post* or the *Enquirer*. For example: "2-BR House 2 Blocks from Beach" might be true, but it doesn't sell the property. "2-BR with 'Wow-Factor Design,'" or "2-BR Retreat in Tropical Paradise" gets attention. The challenge here is coming up with something catchy within the character-limit that has been set by the web site. Have a brainstorming session and get some input from friends and family. What seems obvious to you may make no sense whatsoever to the general public. Writing a headline is relatively easy. Writing a concise and compelling headline—that's another story.

Sunset view from our pool deck. This became the "iconic" scene for our house in Mexico.

Similarly, your write-up on the unit should include descriptive words such as, "beautiful night views; quiet, private setting; fully-equipped kitchen; comfortable living spaces," whatever describes your place in the best light. Mention how far you are located is from the nearest airport, and how long it takes to get from the airport to your house. (Ours was 18 miles from the airport over a two-lane winding road through mountains. 18 miles. 45 minutes. Minimum.)

My advice, however, is not to just talk about what's great about your place, but to give full disclosure in your description. Do not be tempted to lie and say you have ocean views when you have a sliver of a view of the bay. I always discuss the negatives with prospective renters and believe me, reverse psychology works. Our house in Mexico is up the street from a rather poor Mexican neighborhood and if people are walking up the hill, they have to walk past that neighborhood every day. They may drive or take a golf cart up, but they are still going to see the neighborhood. The neighbors are friendly and not threatening, but their living conditions are not at all what many vacationers are used to.

Honesty and full disclosure mean saying things such as:

- We live at the top of a fairly steep hill, otherwise we wouldn't have any views.

- There are a lot of stairs in the house.

- The garden can have mosquitos at night, so bring bug spray.

- There's a flood gate across the entryway to the apartment (as we found at an apartment we rented in Venice, Italy).

Believe me, this will not deter renters who would enjoy your home. It's better to set the right expectations and get a good review than it is to mislead someone, have them be unhappy, go through the stress of hearing their complaints, having them leave early and getting a bad review.

Is your place appropriate for small children? Would people with kids ages five to 10 find the place a good fit? Our house was designed with a pool on the same level as the living room, open stairways, and the second bedroom is a separate building from the main house. It's only about 10 feet away, but there are two exterior doors between them. Toddlers, obviously, were not safe in our house because of the pool and the stairwells. Some parents with children between ages four and 10 were not comfortable with the space between the master bedroom and the second bedroom. Some just brought baby monitors to be sure that if the kids needed them, they could hear them from the master bedroom.

It's critical your rental be a good fit for your renter. It might seem you're going to lose income by putting some renters off, but it doesn't work that way. I often find when I tell someone about a negative, like the neighborhood on the street, it makes them even more determined to rent my place—because they want to experience the "locals."

Good reviews build your business. I figure it takes about a year to get going and collect those reviews, but if you do things right and make sure your renters are a good fit for your property, you'll have good, steady rentals.

Anecdote: Generalizations are just that—generalizations. There are always exceptions. On one occasion we donated a week in the casita to a fundraiser. A lovely young man purchased the week as a gift for his parents, whom we agreed to pick up at the airport as a courtesy. We met Gary and Kathy in arrivals with no problems, but began to get a bit alarmed when she had to stop to rest on the way to the place the car was parked.

Kathy: "I have fibromyalgia," she informed me, "I can't walk far."

Me: "Oh no worries!" (red flag going off in my brain—well, we can get them a golf cart)

By the time we had gotten to the grocery store we had learned the only other vacations they had taken were cruises; Gary had had a heart attack about nine months previously, and she had also had one sometime in the past (they were both a little overweight and they admitted they were out of shape); plus he was just a little bigoted about people of other skin tones.

Cal and I just looked at each other. I think we had simultaneous visions of having to airlift one of them out of Sayulita, home to the hospital in Buffalo. There was nothing about this rental that could be considered a "good fit."

We helped them pick up supplies at the grocery store and Cal got them a golf cart rental, left them to take their naps, crossed our fingers and said a prayer. After the first day we hardly saw them at all. Every day they were off to the beach and out exploring. When we did see them on one of the beaches, there was Gary having a great conversation with an African-American lady sitting next to him. Kathy glowingly reported that this was absolutely the best vacation they had ever had, and the best gift their son could possibly have given them.

Go figure!

A Good Picture Is Worth 1,000 Words—Bad Pictures, Not So Much

You can have a professional photographer take the photos for your web page but you may not want to spend the money. If you are (like me) not prepared to spend money, then prepare to spend time. I can't tell you how many photos I've taken and when I've looked at them there's been some clutter or something in them that looks amiss. Be critical! This is not the time to say, "Well, it's almost perfect." You are competing with web pages which have professional photographs that *are* perfect. They have been professionally staged, professionally lit, and then Photoshopped. I don't know about you, but I have tried to learn Photoshop and definitely—my limits are the editing function in iPhoto. I can crop, lighten or darken, take out a few blemishes and make the colors more intense. I can't remove that crumpled wet towel on the bed or the car in the driveway. I have to begin by taking the shot without the towel or the car.

It's also a good idea to take pictures with a decent camera that produces high resolution photos. I can't tell you how many times I've tried to post a photo and gotten the message "photo is not big enough," meaning it is too small and would be bitmapped (it will have little blocks of color instead of a clear picture) if you did put it on the web site, and the site is not even going to allow you to do that. You can make hi-res photos smaller, but you can't make low-res photos bigger.

- Start by picking a day and time of day when the natural light is good. Clouds will make your place look dark, harsh sunlight might make it too shadowy or stark. Late in the day or early morning on a sunny day are usually best.

- Next, clear the space of clutter. No personal items should show in the photo. You don't have to move everything out of the room, just out of the picture. If you can, "stage" the room. Smooth out all the wrinkles in the beds and make sure the overhang is even and is covering the sheets (at least from the angle you are shooting from). Put a matching throw or possibly neatly folded or rolled, color-matching towels or beach towels at the foot. Make sure the bedside tables are clear. A well-placed book might give a more homey impression; but pill bottles, loose change and pile of magazines will scream "clutter."

- Don't use a wide-angle lens to make your rooms look bigger. As one of my friends (who also rents a house out) says, "It's better to under promise and over deliver."

My pet peeve is looking at a photo of a bedroom where the bed is not nicely made up. A couple of decorative pillows at the head will dress it up a lot. If you are not sure what it should look like, check out some photos online. I love the way the housekeepers in Mexico make a bed. They don't leave a wrinkle to be found, and the color-coordinated towels are artfully folded into the shape of swans or turtles. You don't need to go that far, though, just make sure the bed looks inviting, that's what your guests will be falling into after a long day of travel. They may never make the bed after they get there, but it's the first impression that counts.

- When the "set" is ready, take several pictures from many different angles. That might mean you have to move things after you shoot from one angle to have an uncluttered shot from another angle. Take shots with flash and without flash, with room lights on and with room lights off. Then when you review them, you can choose the ones that make your room look the best. Take notice of the "extras" in view. For example, if there's a doorway in the picture, is that view clear of clutter too? Does the photo look better with the door open or closed? Is the toilet in the bathroom showing when you take the shot of the bedroom? Like I said, this is going to take time!

- When you're doing the dining room or the kitchen, set the table or set out a few wine glasses and a bottle of wine; or something such as cheese and crackers and iced tea on a tray. Again, stage the room so that people can imagine living there and enjoying the space. Choosing a vacation rental is like buying a house. You start with certain criteria, but when you see something that draws you in, it becomes an emotional decision. If you can make your prospects envision the wonderful, relaxing, fun times they will have at your place, you've made the sale.

- Don't take pictures of just a sink, or a shower, or an artistic grouping of pictures or accessories. For good examples of what not to do, check out "For Sale By Owner" listings on Zillow or another realty web site. Some homeowners who are trying to sell on their own get it and post good pictures, but there's a pretty good number who post terrible photos: close-ups of the kitchen sink, the toilet with the seat up, a closet with clothes hanging in it. The idea is not to show people how you live when you're there, but how *they* can live in the space. Give people an idea of the layout of the house, so they can visualize what it would be like to walk through it. Also take pictures of the exterior, grounds of the house/apartment, and of the surrounding scenery. For example, if you live near a beach, get some nice pics of the beach—possibly the sunset. If your place is near mountains, take pictures of the mountains.

Ah yes, a beautiful, Mexican sink—but as lovely as it is—does it really "sell" the unit?

While it may seem time-consuming taking views from different angles, changing the lighting and moving props around, believe me, it's easier to do it when you do the initial shoot. If you are not proficient at Photoshop, it can be very frustrating to have to go back two days later and re-stage the whole room after looking at the pictures on the computer and finding you don't have the shots you need.

On Being a Video Star

Most websites also allow you to upload a video of your home. Videos are even trickier to do than photos. First, supposing you are going to do the video all at once, rather than edit a number of short videos together, you'll have to completely clear away the personal stuff from every room at the same time. Next, there's nothing worse in a video than being swept from one scene to another too quickly. In fact, it can literally be a motion-sickness, nauseating experience. Pan slowly across the room, and make sure you give almost equal time to the majority of the rooms so you aren't jumping from one to the other.

The up side of videos is that they give your prospective renters a walk-through tour of your unit. The downside is that the viewer has to watch the video from beginning to end to get the whole picture. Some renters won't spend the time—they'd prefer to click through photos, where they can come back to the rooms they are specifically interested in. If you want a really good video, you're going to have to hire someone who can light the space, do the recording, and then edit the scenes together. It will be a bit costly. The video might be something you can put off until your rental business is better-established and making some profit.

Adding Photos to the Site in "3 Easy Steps" (Rolling My Eyes Here)

1. Edit your photos in whatever program you use to do that. While you're editing, you can crop out anything extraneous at the edges of the shot—like a half-open door or window; yourself in the mirror, taking the shot; the edge of the toilet. Make sure the photos are on the light side. If there's any chance they are dark, lighten them up as much as possible because on most of the sites I've used, they always look dark once they are uploaded. Uploading is another time-consuming process. It's not fun to get a picture uploaded, see that it's too dark, delete it, go back to your editing program, fix it, and then upload it again. That'll drive you to your "calming" drink pretty quickly!

2. You don't have to upload in the order in which you are going to put the photos on the site, but it will make the job go faster if you have some order to start. When you get them all uploaded and preview how they look, you will probably still change the order somewhat. Think about how people would see your place from the moment they arrive and put the photos in that order. First, the exterior; then, the living area as you walk in the front door; the kitchen; recreation areas (pool, patio, etc.); bedrooms and adjoining baths (master first), and so on.

3. After you have all of your shots uploaded and in the order that makes the most sense, go back and put in some of your scenery shots where they seem to fit best. For example, if there's a view from the living

room, put that view shot in between the living room and the bedroom shots. Beach shots might go after the recreational areas of your house. Use these scenery shots as punctuation, to show places your guests will be able to enjoy when they are staying at your home. Start the photo gallery with your best exterior shot or something that is really appealing—like your pool. End it with a great scenery shot like the beach at sunset.

Autumn shot at a lakeside rental in New York State illustrates the beauty of the environment.

Website Checklists—Oh Boy

Most websites also have checklists for amenities and close-by activities, plus they have maps where they pinpoint the location of your home without giving the address. Take your time to go through these and make sure when you preview your page everything is correct. It's easy to make a slip when you are working on a computer and click on "two" beds when you meant to click "one." (This happened to me—and the consequences were not pretty!) Sometimes you have to actually contact the website to get your "pin" on the map in the correct place. In our case, there were two streets by the same name in the same town—in two completely different "suburbs" (it's a small pueblo in Mexico so I use that term loosely). We had to call the rental web site to get the little balloon pin moved to the right street.

All That Being Said

Most people do not like to read. They look at your pictures, check the number of bedrooms, and look at the rates. So—be prepared to repeat much of your information when you respond to inquiries. Did I say this was a lot of work? This is a lot of work during the seasons that people are most likely to book, which will depend on the time of year in which your "high" season falls.

The clutter-free kitchen counters and dining room table look appealing accented by the art above the counter-opening and a vase of beautiful flowers.

And a Note About the "Preview" Function

All web sites offer you the opportunity to see your page as it will look to the viewer before you publish it. Always use this function frequently and proofread carefully. For the final check, get some fresh eyes—either a family member or friend—to proof for you. Our brains tend to make closure when we've written something or have gone through a checklist, so to us, a sentence might look just right when it's not right at all. It takes someone who hasn't seen it before to catch the mistakes.

Which Web Site—The Choices Can Be Overwhelming

You probably are already aware of the earliest and most popular web sites, Homeaway or VRBO (Vacation Rentals By Owner) and Airbnb, but there are many, many more. Most likely you'll want to use those two well-known names, but remember you'll have to make some decisions based on budget. How much do you want to spend to list your place? Airbnb only charges when you get a booking, VRBO and some other sites charge to list.

The weird thing about web sites is that some work well for certain rentals, and not at all for others. For example, a friend of ours who also has a house in Sayulita, Mexico highly recommends Flipkey and booking.com. I tried both — neither brought us any bookings. Some of the less well-known sites include: WIMDU, Vacasa, The Plum Guide, Innclusive, Kid and Coe, Boutique Homes, and Homestay, to name a few. You might want to google each of these and get a general idea of their target markets to determine if your rental fits their audience, and, of course, what fees they charge.

Anecdote: Owner receives panicked call from renter and house manager, just as owner arrives at her own vacation destination, ready to relax.

Renter (obviously very stressed and in a panic): "There's not enough beds, the web site said there were two queen beds in the master bedroom. I told you Grandma was coming—now there's not enough beds!"

Owner: "How many people does the web site say the house sleeps? It says: six. If there's a mistake in the number of beds in the master bedroom, I'm sorry, that must have been a computer glitch."

Renter: "But I told you grandma would be here in my emails. We discussed this."

Owner, searching through email thread (never delete your emails, keep them all in a separate folder) *while searching her mind for a solution:* "Can we put a couple of the kids up at the hotel just down the street?" *(The hotel can be seen from the house and is no more than a 3-minute walk down the road)*

Renter: "That would totally ruin the vacation. The idea was that Grandma would have some time to spend with the kids!" *(Note: Said "kids" are 15, 17, and 18-year-olds. We all know how much time they want to spend with Grandma.)*

Owner finds email: "It says here, 'Grandma is coming from Puerto Vallarta for one night and she can bunk in with the girls.' My assumption* (we all know how foolish that is), *since you asked for the king bed in the second bedroom* *instead of two twins, was that for one night, Grandma would sleep with the girls in that bed."*

Renter: "Well, she's here for three nights and this won't do, our whole vacation is spoiled!"

Owner, trying to keep calm: "Instead of panicking over this, let's figure out a solution. There's an extra mattress that is not being used in another unit. We can bring that up and one of the kids can sleep on it on the floor."

Renter: "Okay—I guess."

Upshot of this situation: The web page was wrong about the queen beds, it had rolled over to two beds instead of one—so watch what happens when you use those "rolling choose the number dials"—however, the renter did understand the site said the house slept six, not seven. Grandma stayed nine nights, not three and the site also said, "extra guests will be charged $25/night," which was never charged to the renter. This group also used every towel, sheet and blanket in the house and left their clothes lying around to such an extent that when the housecleaner came to clean (twice, at no extra charge), she was unable to do laundry because she couldn't uncover the washer and dryer. When I returned, grandma had done two loads of laundry, the housecleaner had done four loads, and I did seven loads myself.

Moral: You can't win 'em all! It is inevitable you will have some negative experiences, but just as a caution—in my experience, large groups with teenagers have been the most challenging, probably because most teenagers tend to leave things right where they drop when they are done *with them. (Just thinking about it I'm having flashbacks of my kids' rooms when they were teens.)*

And—A Few Words About Your Own Web Page/Social Media Site

If you really want to market your place from multiple venues, you can purchase a domain name from one of the online templet-based sites and create your own site. This generally works best after you've developed your business a bit. You will eliminate paying booking fees to the home-sharing sites, however, your potential renters may want to negotiate a better price, based on the fact they aren't going through a site that's charging you fees. You can also do Facebook, Instagram, Twitter—any and all of the other social media options. This is a great way to keep in touch with renters who have been to your place previously. Keeping your place at the top of their minds will help keep them coming back. But again, you have to commit the time to continually updating these sites so there's always fresh information going out.

There is no question having your own site and doing social media takes a lot of time, so you have to make the commitment. Remember, the rule of thumb for small businesses is that you spend one day a week—20 percent of your time—on marketing.

The CALENDAR

If you're on more than one site, you will very quickly learn why this word is in capital letters. Keeping all of your calendars coordinated and up-to-date can be a major headache. Some sites tell you they sync with other sites so when you make a booking on their end it is automatically blocked off on your other calendar(s). This may work, or it may not. When I tried it, one site automatically blocked all of my dates on the other site. Obviously, this would mean you're losing business from site two, and also, since renters often look at your place on more than one site, it's confusing to them. Is the place booked for their dates or isn't it?

In any event, you should check *all* of your calendars (I always keep one on my computer as well) when you make a booking to ensure you aren't double-booked. When you're doing bookings, focus on the number of nights people are staying, not the number of days. They arrive, for example: May 1, and leave May 8. That's seven nights *and* the night of the 8th is available to be rented if you are able to turn over the unit within a day.

Which leads us to: setting check-in and check-out times. The home-sharing web sites have an option to state what time you allow people to come in and what time you need them to leave. When they are making their travel plans, however, people take whatever flight time works best for them. You have to decide how much you are willing and able to accommodate guests' arrival and departure times. It can be very helpful to have a secure place for people to store their suitcases until a unit is ready for them, or until they have to catch their ride to the airport.

Anecdote: A word about those calendars. More than once I had people make an inquiry where the automated part of the system gave dates they had used for prior bookings, not the time period they actually wanted. The first time, the email inquiry gave certain dates and in the message-box, the renter asked for some specifics that showed he thought he was coming to Palm Springs—not Mexico. I wrote back explaining our house was in Mexico, not Palm Springs. The client quickly realized the system had used his message from a booking he had made in Palm Springs over a year ago.

The second time, a couple were planning to spend the first four weeks of the winter in San Miguel de Allende, and the following four weeks with us in Sayulita. Unfortunately, their inquiry gave the dates for the San Miguel booking. That one was a bit of a hash-up, since I accepted the inquiry and then they had two bookings for the same dates, and no booking for the dates they needed in Sayulita. When all was said and done, we were doubled-booked their first night, so we had to put them up in our second bedroom—but they did become friends and we've maintained contact to this day.

Chapter 2

Hit 'Em Between the Eyes

What your renters see when they first walk through the door of your space will significantly influence their feelings about the place. A friend of mine whose family rents the same cottage on Lake Erie every year said: "The place is not fancy, the furniture is old, and it's not even particularly clean, but every year we walk in to see a vase of fresh flowers on the table and it just makes a very welcoming impression."

I agree, fresh flowers are a great touch, but this book is called "Host for the MOST"—meaning what can you do to attract the most rentals and get the highest rates for your particular unit and area—which is why I'm going to go into a lot more detail on what to do to make your place make a great first, and second impression.

Looks count for a lot, but that doesn't mean I'm not an advocate of cleanliness—as you will see later on, I'm a clean freak—however, a little extra effort on the "looks" part is a good place to start.

First the Basics

Guests understand that not everyone can have great furniture; however, you can have great accessories without spending a lot of money. This doesn't mean clutter— people bring their own clutter with them and they need a place to put it. What I mean by accessories is:

- COLOR and PATTERN-COORDINATED decorative pillows and throws will disguise a couch or chair that has seen better days.

- Matching bedspreads, area rugs, sheets and towels (you may want to go with white on the sheets and towels, depending on your location and the number of guests you have).

- Some appealing (err on the conservative side — nothing that might offend) artwork on the walls (hung at the average person's eye level, not the eye level of the Jolly Green Giant).

- Lamps that light up the places people want to sit at night and read.

- A few useful accessories such as coasters and candles in case the electricity goes out or people want to add a little romantic ambience. They should feel free to light these candles so they can be already used, but no matter what, they should be clean. Candles that are covered with dust give the message they are just there for decoration. There's a debate (Can you believe people worry about such things?) about scented vs. unscented candles. My husband likes scented, but if you are making a meal the scent will interfere with the delicious odors of your meal, so you may want to have some unscented options.

If you don't have an eye for this kind of thing (and many people don't, so you are not alone), ask a friend who does to help you, check out some magazines, or the HGTV channel. If your place is by a lake, or the ocean, or in the middle of a forest, try to stick with a theme that goes with the setting. That will set some parameters so you don't go hog wild on everything in the store that looks like it *might* go in your place.

Another way to set parameters is to limit your color scheme in your rooms to three shades that go well together, such as taupe, red and black; orange, lime and yellow; turquoise, grey and navy—you get the picture, there are endless combinations. In our ski chalet near Buffalo (bet you didn't know Buffalo had ski resorts) we went for warm and cozy rich reds, greens and taupes. Our beach house, on the other hand, was all light shell pinks and turquoises, with a few bright accessories to bring in the Mexican theme.

You can mix and match patterns if the colors follow one theme—even in B&W you get the idea.

Stop by a paint store, Lowe's or Home Depot and pick up some brochures; or start with an article you really like—a decorative pillow, a piece of art, a rug or a duvet cover. The three-color scheme doesn't mean you have only the exact same three colors everywhere, you have shades of the same three colors, variations on the theme. (Make a note: This rule works also well for planning a wardrobe on a limited budget or are dealing with limited storage space like the carry-on suitcase you are taking for your one-month trip. Everything goes with everything else if you limit your color scheme to three.)

If you're like me and want some variety, you'll want to do different rooms in different colors. Try to have colors that are related to one another, however, so that one room flows into the next. For example, if you have a summer place and you want a light, airy look, choose light shades of grey, blues, beige, or off whites throughout. If you have a winter getaway and you want a more cozy feel, go for darker, richer jewel tones such as taupes, greens or blues.

There are so many discount home accessory stores now—HomeGoods, T.J. Maxx, Marshalls, Ross, World Market, Stein Mart, Ikea and Kohl's to name a few—it can be daunting. The key to shopping discount is: don't go in the store looking for a great deal on one specific item. You might need sheets or towels or pillows, so yes, you can go specifically for that type of furnishing. But if you need throw pillows or rugs or bedspreads, you might not find the right thing at the right price at the first store you go into—or even the first time you're out shopping for those items. Price is just as important to me as whether things match. (There's a reason I'm married to the "Curmudgeon" as we lovingly call him.) I usually have a price point in mind, and anything I buy has to be in close range of that dollar amount or I won't buy it—no matter how beautiful it is or how well it goes in my house.

When you absolutely have to have something that matches a look you have already established in the house and you don't have the time to shop around several stores, you can look online and usually find what you need at a good price. Again, there are so many online options, Amazon, Overstock, Wayfair, Houzz, WestElm, to name a few. Otherwise, it's a "keep your eyes" open game whenever you're in a store, and you'll find yourself outfitting your space with some really great bargains.

The first place I look when I get in one of these stores is the clearance shelf. Some stores even have sales that include discounts on the goods that are already on clearance. I have paid 50 cents for placemats that started at $8, $18 for a $60 queen size duvet set, $5 for a beautiful throw to go on a couch. You do have to be a shopper, but if you are furnishing a rental and you want it to look good without spending a lot of money, it can be done.

FYI—Even if you have lots of money, you don't want to spend a lot. Renters will respect your place more when they see you have taken the time and made the effort to have it look good—but it's still not their place and they are on vacation. They will have accidents, break dishes, and get stains on things. You will have to replace rental property furnishings much more often than you replace the things you have at home, especially if someone else is doing the cleaning. Housekeepers don't spend a lot of time getting stains out of sheets, make-up off of facecloths, or wiping candle wax off of the candle holders or floors. They have a job to do and then they move on to the next place they have to clean.

Anecdote: Just a quick candle story. At one time I took a trip to New York City with a boyfriend and we stayed at one of those really cool brownstones in Brooklyn. Basically, we were renting a large bedroom, with the bathroom out in the hallway. There were dozens of taper candles placed all around the room, each in its own ornate candelabra. It was, after all, supposed to be a romantic getaway, so I wanted to light the candles. What else were they there for? My companion, however, was not so sure we should. The homeowners, who lived downstairs were older and kind of staid-looking. Even though they had candles all over, they didn't look as though they were the type to connect candles with the concept of romance.

Being a bit headstrong, one evening I lit several candles— maybe a dozen out of the 40 that were there. Although the effect was beautiful, the final outcome was not. My friend received a rather nasty email saying the owners had collected those candles over many years (really?) and they should not have been used—and a fee for the used candles was deleted from our damage deposit.

One Room at a Time—Starting with the Living Room

Living room—no clutter, but looks comfortable and has some inviting art work on the walls.

This could be a living room, great room, or the bedroom/living area of a studio, or maybe it's the single room you are renting. It should be freshly swept or vacuumed and dusted. Most people think dusting means swiping a cloth around a table top. I am allergic to dust, as are many other people, so I try to think of it as "dust removal." This means you don't just move things around on the table top, you dust them too. Dust lamps and lampshades, dust knick-knacks, dust TVs, ceiling fans, pictures. I find the quickest, most effective way to do this is with one of those fake feather dusters. I add a little something to make the dust cling even better, and then I (or the housecleaner if you can afford one) can whip through.

As we discussed under "accessories"—the space should look appealing because you've tried to give it some homey touches. If there's a bookshelf, leave a selection of books the guests may want to read in case they run out of their own reading materials. A coffee table is a great place to put some publications that highlight the tourist attractions near you, a map or two and your "Renters Book." The Renters Book gets its own chapter, more later …

What do guests need for furnishings in living space? They need at least a couple of reasonably comfortable chairs to sit in and enjoy the evenings, a coffee or side table, a reading lamp, and possibly an ottoman. In Europe, space is limited so two chairs for a two-person rental might be all you can fit. In Western countries, where houses are generally more spacious, a couch and a chair, a coffee table, side tables and reading lamps should fill most people's needs.

It doesn't matter who they are or where they are from, 99.9 percent of your guests will want WiFi. We live in an age where we just can't seem to separate ourselves from the grid. Americans tend to touch base with their work while they are on vacation. Folks from other countries want to be able to phone or FaceTime family and friends. You need to have the most reliable WiFi you can provide. Of course, we all know that WiFi and the Internet are not infallible, especially in second world countries, and when it goes off, you are sure to hear about it from your renters. That's why you want to get the best you can—why have to handle any more issues than absolutely necessary? Save your sanity!

I still believe television is optional in a vacation property, but that's because I can't imagine sitting in my room watching TV while I'm on Holiday. Even if the weather is bad, there are usually places to see and things to explore, no matter where you are.

I realize, though, that not everyone agrees with me on this. It seems young people especially, like to have TV. What we have done is provided television screens, DVD players, and a selection of DVDs. You do want a television screen that has a port for the connector to a computer. If the renter has access to online streaming services and brings their own connector, they can then stream programs over WiFi. If you want to provide a connector (or a Firestick, Roku or other streaming device), just be aware that those are the things that tend to develop legs and walk off. Electricity converters and flashlights are the same story. I can't tell you how many flashlights we put in our units, and somehow they either found their way into someone's suitcase or got lost at a beach party.

Deciding whether or not to provide TV will depend on your location and your market. You may have to pay for cable or a satellite dish if your renters need full-service television. (Keep in mind that not many people consistently watch network TV these days.) There are less expensive options that will get you the basic channels in form of compact digital antennae that work just fine. One place we visited had an antenna located in a picture frame that was placed on a windowsill. It did a great job of bringing in the standard U.S. stations: CBS, ABC, NBC and Fox.

Now this is a pretty basic place—it's a Park Model trailer at a lake resort. When the owners bought the trailer it was 19 years old so what furnishings were there were ready for the trash. They didn't want to spend a lot, however, so a basic "Klic-Klac" futon couch, colorful pillows, reading lamps on side tables, a small ottoman that doubled as a coffee table and side chairs that could be used outdoors fit the bill—all for about $1,500 from Raymour & Flanagan and HomeGoods. The accessories on the shelf above the window add a homey touch.

Anecdote: As usual, it's 11 o'clock my time, when a frantic email arrives from a renter who is staying in the casita for her daughter's wedding. The WiFi at the house is not working, so she has had to go to the "big house" where the wedding party is staying to use theirs, and this is not acceptable. (Note: there are many cafes and restaurants that have WiFi). I'm 3,600 miles away and am paying a house manager fairly good money to resolve these issues. I ask if she has talked to him. She has. He has called the WiFi provider, but they only work in the daytime—and, it is Mexico after all. Service people are not likely to show up in a few hours—in fact, if you want them at all, the best thing to do is snag them when you see them on the street and hand them $200 pesos (Mexican).

It didn't take me long (not as long as it took the service guy to come), to figure out that this renter was not as upset with the lack of WiFi as she was with the idea of having to be at the big wedding house because she had just gone through a bad divorce—and that was where her ex was—with his new wife.

Chapter 3

If You Aren't Mr(s). Fix-it, Hire One

Here is a typical, Murphy's Law real-life situation:

Guests are about to arrive for the house, in maybe five minutes. My husband, Cal, is trying all of the keys in the locks to make sure he's giving them the right ones. He inserts a key into a particularly challenging lock, and it gets stuck. Really stuck! It's the wrong key. The door is open and the bolt is extended in the "lock" position, so now you can't even close the door all the way, let alone close it and lock it. He runs to his tool box, takes out the hammer and gets the key out, but the bolt is still stuck. The guests arrive while he is screwing the lock body off, removing it, fixing the bolt, and screwing it back on. My husband really is a Mr. Fix-it and his talent for that has been our salvation on more than one occasion.

Hosting for short- (and even long-term) rentals is the one case where you should "sweat the small stuff." If you want to get good reviews, your guests will expect EVERYTHING to work properly. This means you or your house manager needs to go through the house before new guests arrive with a checklist:

- Are all the light bulbs working? Replace any that aren't.

- Are the handles on the faucets on tightly? Do any of the sinks drip?

- Does the air conditioner remote control work? For that matter, does the A/C work?

- Are all of the door knobs on securely?

- Do all of the locks work?

- Do all windows open and close properly? In some climates where there's a lot of humidity you might have some that get stuck and can't be fixed during the rainy season, but at least point out the ones that are not working to guests.

- Does the microwave, stove, toaster, kettle, coffeemaker, etc. work properly?

- Do the fans work?

- Are there any "tricks" in your unit—such as, if you run the microwave and the toaster at the same time, will the circuit breaker go off? If so, leave a sign telling renters not to run them both at once. If a circuit does go out, where is the circuit breaker and should the renters switch it themselves or call the house manager?

- Does a patch of wall need to be scraped and painted?

- Are there any broken chair legs?

- Is there hot water?

- Is there a nest of bees under the chairs on the terrace? (If there is, I can guarantee it will be your guest's sweet grandma who becomes the target—at least it was at our casita.)

Make signs for the things you want to remind your renters of, and label the light switches. It may seem a little weird living with little framed signs saying, "Please use the cutting boards," "Please do not put anything except toilet paper in the toilet," and having labels on your light switches stating what light the switch turns on, but the signs are necessary for reminding renters of the rules (and can save you a lot of grief and expenses down the road), and the labels are a big help to people who are not familiar with your house.

If something breaks, either fix it or throw it out—or, if you can't bear to throw it out because it "might come in handy someday"—put it away somewhere guests won't see it. I can't tell you how many times I've argued with my spouse about getting rid of something (he tends to hoard, I tend to clean out) and sure enough, months or years down the road that something has provided useful parts or been reused.

If you can't use a screwdriver, a hammer, and a paintbrush or light the pilot light on a hot water tank or a furnace, then you need to find a reliable handyman or house manager who can. I have had so many emails at 11 o'clock at night (my time)—there's no hot water. Or, a review, "the casita was delightful but we didn't have any hot water the whole week we were there." Hello! Cold showers are not the norm, even in Mexico. Plus, this is usually an easy fix.

Your Tool Box

You will need to leave a basic tool box somewhere that the house manager and even the guests can get at. It'll be convenient for you too—when the key gets stuck in the lock. Here's a list of common tools and replacement items you'll need (Be prepared to replace these fairly frequently. When other people use your stuff, some of it will disappear.):

- Hammer

- Flat head and Phillips head screw drivers, large and small

- Small case of various sizes of Allen wrenches
- Needle-nosed pliers
- Medium-sized wrench
- Long-nosed lighter for pilot lights
- Extension cord
- Light bulbs
- Guts for toilets
- Washers for any faucets that take them

Anecdote: Morning call from upstairs renter in Buffalo, NY, our hometown: "I don't have any hot water." A check of his hot water tank reveals that it is shot and needs to be replaced. About an hour later, email from gentlemen renters staying at vacation house. "We haven't had hot water since we've been here (a week) and we'd like to take hot showers before we go home to our wives today." (Note: In their initial inquiry, these two fellows asked what kind of a discount would I give "to two old codgers looking to escape from their wives for a week.")

Owner (3,600 miles away): "But you have two units. NEITHER of the hot water tanks are working?"

Renter: "No."

Owner: "Why didn't you call the house manager?"

Renter: "Oh, we tried to get him this morning (it's Sunday), his wife said he's gone surfing."

Owner, trying not to sound too frustrated: "Why didn't you let him know earlier this week? It's probably just the pilot lights—which is usually an easy fix. If not, we're having really bad hot water tank karma today—we're replacing one here. I can't believe three hot water tanks could go on the same day! When do you have to leave?"

Renter: "The taxi is coming in an hour."

Solution: *Two old codgers go home to their wives after having yet another cold shower.*

Chapter 4

A Good Night's Sleep Is Worth a Thousand Bucks—A Bad One Is Worth a Bad Review

Typically, by the time travelers get to your house, they've been traveling for at least six to 12 hours. First of course, they want to eat and likely have their favorite refreshment: a beer, glass of wine, or whatever that might be. Then all they can think about is a clean, comfortable bed that they can flop into and get a good night's rest.

Good sleep depends on a number of things: quiet, darkness, and comfort. Some things you can control—others, not so much! If you can't guarantee there won't be barking dogs, street noise or roosters crowing in the morning, focus on the things you can control (For the noises you can't control—such as the roosters, dogs and the neighbor's loud muffler—the answer is usually ear plugs. If you are in a position to provide them, which means you live near your rental and check it yourself so you can replenish the supply, then tell renters you have them. If check-ins and handling of guests are left up to a house manager, you're better off to suggest light sleepers bring their own ear plugs.):

- Someplace to set luggage to unpack: this can be a low table, or an actual foldable luggage rack. Some travelers will be living out of their open suitcase, so this is really an essential.

- The mattress: This is an area where you can't please all of the people all of the time, so try to strike a happy medium. Invest in a relatively firm mattress, and if your mattresses are more than 10 years old and you rent your place a lot, get new ones. Lumps and sags are not welcome surfaces for todays' travelers. For most of us, there's nothing worse than getting through the night on a mattress where you're continually rolling into your sleep partner.

- Pillows: One of the highest compliments I've ever received in a review was, "the house had great pillows." (I know, I am kind of crazy, right?) Pillows need to be replaced approximately every year and a half. They are not hugely expensive items, folks. Again, you need to find that happy medium between soft and firm, but flat as a pancake is not acceptable. At least give them something they can punch up. Beds look better made up with four pillows, two in pillow cases and two in shams, plus a couple of smaller decorative throw pillows.

- Mattress and pillow covers: Ideally you are going to purchase bedbug-proof mattress and pillow covers that zip up so it's like putting the mattress in an envelope. Bedbugs? Ewwww, not in my house— you say! Bedbugs have made a big comeback recently. People actually pick them up from rooms while they are traveling and bring them along in their suitcases. They aren't easy to get rid of once they get into a mattress, so the best defense is good offense. Get the bedbug covers—you can find them online. Then put a decent quality mattress cover over the top of the bedbug cover to protect it and make it more comfortable. Some of the bedbug covers are made of plastic, which is not very comfortable to sleep on and are the reason you need a decent mattress pad over top. Ditto for the pillow covers. It's always good to have cotton mattress and pillow covers so you can bleach them if they get stained.

- Sheets: Good quality, high thread count, plain-colored sheets. I love colors, but white can be bleached and, if you or your cleaner pours laundry detergent directly on colored sheets the color will come out, leaving the sheet looking like it's stained (ditto for colored towels). Patterned sheets are generally lower thread count, and if you are not the one making up the bed all of the time you can end up with some pretty interesting and not very appealing combinations of patterns. Plain is a safer bet. You should have three sets of sheets for each bed, although to start you can make do with two. The idea is: one set on the bed, one set in the laundry, and one extra in case someone gets sick.

- How often you wash sheets and towels is between you and the guests. You can automatically launder both a couple of times a week, or ask your guests if they want their sheets and towels changed every couple of days or once a week. Those who are more conscious of the environment will most likely opt to keep the same sheets and towels for a week's visit. Most people do not change their beds or their towels more than once a week at home. (Okay, so there are exceptions to every generalization. I confess I do have friends who use a clean towel every time they bathe. They never had kids, though.)

- Duvet covers and shams: These don't need to be washed every time the sheets are changed but they should be washed every time there's a turnover in guests. You might like bedspreads, but here's what I do: I use empty duvet covers (no duvets necessary) instead of spreads because they can be quickly and easily washed and dried. I have two sets, one for the bed and one for the laundry. Needless to say—these should be decorative and match the room.

- Blankets: Depending on climate, you will need to provide an appropriate blanket for each bed. The lighter-weight, quick dry is the best, because these really should also be washed between guests. These don't necessarily have to match everything else, neutral colors will do. (*Once, when we were in Mexico for Thanksgiving and my daughter was there helping with the seasonal clean up, I asked her to gather up all the blankets so I could wash them. "Mom," she said. "It's 85 degrees out!" —"Nathalie, it's November. Winter is coming—even though we are in the tropics!"*)

- Rugs: It's just nice to have at least a small rug on each side of the bed so when people get up they are not stepping on cold floors in bare feet. Color-coordinate these to the bed covers. Ikea has inexpensive ones that dry quickly when washed, but check out the discount stores too.

- Lighting: Bedside lamps are a must, even with today's e-readers. Ikea has some very inexpensive table models ($8–$10), or check out the thrift shops near you.

- Decorative hooks: When you are traveling it is so much easier to hang something on a hook than to put it back in a suitcase. Using drawers or cupboards can be stressful because when you leave, OMG, did you check each and every one to make sure you didn't forget something? HOOKS—think about it—cheaper than dressers or armoires and easier to use.

Doesn't this bed look inviting with its fluffy pillows and soft rug at the side? The bench at the foot can double as a suitcase stand.

Anecdote: One of our trips involved a stay at a B&B in British Columbia close to a lake where my sister and her husband had a summer place. The B&B looked okay and had all the necessary licenses, but we didn't check out the reviews because there weren't a lot of accommodation options in the area. When we got there, we found it was owned by a couple who had originally owned a farm in one of the prairie provinces of Canada. Typical of farmers in their generation, they had a very large family, now all grown. When they retired and moved to B.C., they bought a two-story raised ranch with about five bedrooms on the first floor, where their B&B guests stayed.

They were a lovely couple, but I'm pretty sure all of the mattresses were the originals from the farm. There wasn't anyone else there so they told us to take whichever room we wanted. Well, we must have tried seven or eight beds (there was more than one bed per room). It was not an easy choice figuring out which one had the fewest springs popping out of it, and the least lumps and sags.

We didn't get a good night's sleep, but the farm breakfast the next morning was incredible! It was more than the two of us could ever eat, with homemade cinnamon rolls and jellies, eggs, Canadian bacon, coffee, pancakes and fresh-squeezed orange juice. Facing this feast, thoughts of the bed and the poor night's sleep faded. The moral of the story is, if you can't provide a great breakfast that will erase the memory of a terrible mattress—opt for a new mattress.

Cleaning Services

Between guests, you will want to give the bedroom a fairly thorough cleaning: dusting all surfaces, vacuuming rugs, washing floors, and changing the sheets—be sure you get under the bed, any dressers and tables. If you have guests staying for a week, it's good to offer cleaning at least once during their stay. Some hosts prefer to have the maid or cleaner come daily, however this can be a bit disruptive to guests. It's your call and—if you are not charging an extra fee for cleaning—it's your money. You have to set your nightly rate to cover the cost of the service.

Many places do charge an extra fee for cleaning, which is a non-negotiable requirement, because it covers the cleaning between guests. I have had many prospective renters offer to do their own cleaning if I would lower the rental fee. If they had seen the endless meters of tile floors that had to be swept and mopped, I'm sure they wouldn't have even thought of cleaning the place themselves.

Personally, I'm not a fan of add-on fees. When the guest is researching places to stay, the first quote they get is the per-night price, which they then multiply by the number of nights they plan to stay. That can make your place look pretty reasonable until the cleaning fee and taxes are added in. All of a sudden, the price is beyond their budget. If the cost of cleaning is covered in the nightly fee, the renter gets a more realistic feel for the cost of their stay.

Laundry

Most hosts have a washer/dryer on the premises because it's usually easier to do the laundry while you're cleaning than take it out. In places like Mexico, however, wash, dry and fold services are common and inexpensive, so they are always good for a back-up if you or your housecleaner get behind.

When you buy a new washer/dryer, you'll want to get the largest capacity you can afford, especially if your home sleeps several people. Many people like front-loading washing machines, which are generally more expensive than top-loaders. Do your own research, but generally the front-loaders are considered to save water and electricity, so it might be the better bargain for you in the long run. In some second-world countries, water is a big concern. We had a huge cistern in our garage, but during the Holiday Season and Easter we were guaranteed to run out of water so we'd have to order a truck load. That's when the laundry services in town really came in handy. It's generally preferable to have water for your guests to shower and flush the toilets, rather than water for laundry.

There's a lot to be said in favor of laundry services that not only wash and dry your sheets, but also iron them. If you have access to one and can afford it, you and your guests will love the results.

There's usually a place on home-sharing web sites to check off if you have a washer/dryer guests can use, but often that's one of the questions guests ask whether you've check "yes"or "no." Our policy was not to allow them to use laundry because the house was rented frequently and the washer and dryer got a pretty good work-out just doing sheets, towels and beach towels. We wanted these appliances to last as long as possible, so we didn't have to absorb the cost of replacing them. Since we didn't allow people to use the laundry, we told them exactly where to take their clothes for the wash/dry and fold services (clearly stated in the "Renters Book"), and how much it would cost (about $2 a load), and most were happy with that. Who wants to spend your vacation doing laundry, anyway?

We did make some exceptions for guests who stayed longer or had younger children, but most of the time, the washer and dryer were locked up. You might think this is stingy, but I have a daughter who wears something for two hours, takes it off and puts it in the wash … if you get those kinds of guests, it could be a lot of wear and tear on your appliances, a high electric bill and the possibility of running out of water.

A Note About Materials/Fabrics

The quality of the fabrics you choose for sheets, bed covers, mattress covers, rugs, etc. will determine how often you have to replace these items. If you are planning to have same-day turnovers (someone checks out and new guests check in on the same day), choose materials that dry quickly. Even if you don't need to wash and immediately re-use a set of sheets or a duvet cover, you don't want to have leftover laundry still in the dryer when new guests arrive. An extra spin in the washer will help things dry more quickly, but thicker fabrics take longer to dry. I had one mattress cover that looked so lovely and comfortable because it was heavily padded, but when I washed it, it was a two-day ordeal to get it dry. I usually had to hang it over the terrace rail in the sun to finish it up because otherwise I would have had to run the dryer for hours.

Anecdote: The argument over pillows—Husband: "Why do we need to buy new pillows, it seems like we just bought them!" Wife: "Because they are getting flat and are stained (even with pillow covers on them—they are being used in a hot, humid climate)."

Husband (as I think I mentioned earlier—who is very frugal and is also lovingly known by the nickname "the Curmudgeon"): "Well, why can't we just get two instead of four, they don't use the ones that are in the pillow shams."

Wife: "Because they do use the ones in the pillow shams and besides, when the maid changes the bed, she doesn't keep specific pillows for the shams and others for the pillows."

Solution: Wife googles, "the lifetime of a pillow" and finds the recommended time period is 18 months. Then, when she buys new pillows, she marks the date on them with a laundry marker. Extreme differences of opinion call for extreme measures.

Chapter 5

Bathrooms, Where Indeed, "Cleanliness Is Next to Godliness"

Since bathrooms are very expensive to upgrade, you are probably stuck with the existing bath even though it might have ancient pink tile and a shower so small you can barely raise your arms to shampoo your head. This is a case of working with what you have. The first thing in a bathroom is that it should be immaculately clean. When you start off, this may mean scrubbing moldy grout or calcified taps with a toothbrush. But look at it this way—elbow grease is free, whereas new taps and grout will cost you big time (unless of course, you are Mr. & Mrs. Moneybucks—but then, why are you renting out your space when you could be basking in the sun on some Riviera?).

If you have the funds, you can spruce an old bathroom up with new faucets, light fixtures, hardware on the vanity, outlets and light plates, and possibly some storage shelves. Make sure there's an outlet for an electric razor, blow dryer or electric toothbrush.

After you've cleaned, the next step is—you guessed it—a trip to the discount stores for towels (at least two sets), shower curtains and rugs that MATCH each other and complement the gaudy pink tile (or whatever you have). In the West, we have this eccentric habit of using facecloths. That is not the norm in most European or Latin American countries, but if you are doing a rental and expect to have American guests, it's a good idea to add them to your lists. Most of us Westerners who travel realize there can be a scarcity of facecloths, so we bring them with us. It's not easy, however, to pack them when they are wet, so we appreciate it if they are supplied.

To really impress, your shopping list should include:

- A night light so people can find their way to the bathroom in the dark.

- Shelves (if they are not already there) for people to put their gear on.

- Nice soap dispenser and wastepaper basket.

- A mat for the bathtub or shower so people don't slip and fall when it's wet (this is a liability issue—so essential).

- A make-up mirror that lights up. Ninety percent of the time, bathrooms are poorly lit and it is impossible to do a decent job with make-up—and not ALL of us are natural beauties!

- A blow-dryer.

- Towel racks or some kind of towel hangers.

- Decorative hooks for people to hang their clothes or pajamas on while they shower.

- A small first aid kit with the essentials: bandaids, disinfectant, aspirin, anti-diarrhea.

- Body wash and shampoo—I like to supply these and body wash makes more sense than a bar of soap that has to be thrown out after one set of guests uses it. You can supply the small sample bottles like the ones you get in hotels, but this is definitely pricier than the family-size you can buy at Costco.

Once you have it all put together, it's pretty easy to keep the bathroom up; just clean it thoroughly between guests. Check inside the cupboards once in awhile to make sure they are clean, and take a look to see you're not running low on body wash, shampoo, etc. Go over the towels and rugs once in awhile to make sure they aren't getting threadbare from washing. Wash the shower curtains, since water often discolors the bottom of these, and check that your non-slip mat is not getting moldy. If it is, you'll probably need to take some bleach to it, unless you want to buy a new one.

Anecdote: My husband and I rented a small apartment in Venice that was within our budget of $100 per night (You can still do Italy on $100/night!). The bedroom looked really cute and bright in the pictures and it was in a great location, a real Venetian neighborhood, close to the Vaporetto (water bus). Although "the Curmudgeon" gets around pretty well, he has had two knee replacements and a back fusion, so he's not what you would describe as "spry."

Upon our arrival we found that we had to step over a flood gate (not mentioned or shown in the description online) at the entrance to the apartment. The apartment itself is right on a canal and is charming because the gondolas go past the kitchen window, but the entrance is only six feet from said canal, which can be counted on to flood at least once a year. Inside there was another small flood gate, maybe 14-inches high, right at the doorway to the bathroom, which was divided again into two sections. The first section contained a very small sink and the ubiquitous bidet (Nearly every bathroom in Europe has one, but sorry—typically Americans don't use them and fail to see the wisdom in having one.), then there was a small raised ledge between the bidet and the toilet and the shower. Yes, like an RV. So when you took a shower the toilet got wet.

We ended up loving the place because it so had the feel of Medieval Italy, was close to transportation and restaurants, and it did have all of the basics that we needed. It was just a bit tricky getting in and out of the apartment, particularly for Cal, keeping the toilet paper dry, and going to the bathroom in the middle of the night. #wishIbroughtmyownnightlight!

Chapter 6

The Kitchen—Cook's Delight or Hell's Kitchen

Different vacationers need very different things in a kitchen. Generally, short-term renters staying one week or less will not cook a lot. They prefer to go out and enjoy their time off. This is why short-term renters are actually a bonus for owners. They don't cause a lot of wear and tear on the place.

Long-term renters, and some short-term people, will do a lot more cooking. Some folks just love to cook, and those people appreciate a well-equipped kitchen. Like bathrooms, kitchens are very expensive to renovate, so in most cases, you're going to have to make do with what you have.

Also like bathrooms, start with cleanliness. Sinks, faucets, inside of cabinets, stoves, refrigerators and floors will look better if they are thoroughly cleaned, no matter how old they are. A cheap and easy way to update a kitchen is to paint the cabinets. You'd be surprised what a difference it will make. Appliances can also be spray painted. When our fridge in Mexico started to rust because of the humidity and salt in the air from the ocean, I picked up some sand paper and spray appliance paint. It didn't last forever, but it made a better impression than the rust.

Some cheap but chic updates for kitchens include:

- New hardware on the cupboards and drawers
- Stick-on decals for old tile backsplashes
- New light fixtures
- New light switches and outlet plates

- If you don't have a lot of counter space and have a little room, one of those small stand-alone islands to provide more drawers, shelves and space to cook

- New faucets

If the floors are bad, some colorful throw rugs or rubber mats can cover up the worn spots, plus they make it easier for the cook and clean up crew to stand while they are working. Once again, try to match things up: dishes, dish towels, rugs, kitchen accessories.

Mini-kitchens are fine if your place is small and you are not looking to attract long-term renters. Try to provide shelving if the kitchen is compact and doesn't have a lot of counter space. People need places to put the food they are going to cook. A mini-kitchen should include:

- Small refrigerator.

- Microwave.

- Coffeemaker and filters.

- Electric tea kettle.

- Minimum two of these: cups, plates, cereal bowls, water glasses, wine glasses, sets of cutlery. Place settings for four save guests from having to wash the dishes each time they eat, but you may not have room to store all of that. (Those bamboo dish racks can be used to store dishes on a counter so you don't need a cupboard to put them in.)

- A corkscrew, bottle opener and can opener.

- A couple of sharp knives, a knife sharpener, and serving implements.

- A supply of paper towels.

- A sink to rinse things in, plus dish detergent.

- A sponge and a dish towel.

- A small drying rack or one of those mats for the counter.

You might want to throw in a toaster (or toaster oven if you have space), and a small table and chairs so your guests can sit down and eat.

Going from the basics for a mini-kitchen to a real cook's kitchen requires a little more planning. Good cooks find two things are absolutely necessary: sharp knives and good pans. It's difficult to turn out a good meal without these basics. There's an endless list of kitchen accessories that make cooking easier, but here's my list of essentials:

- Large, medium frypans; 1-quart and 2-quart saucepans; one big pot for boiling spaghetti or making soup. Calphalon has a reputation for being one of the best, but it's expensive, and guests are certain to scrape up the interiors on the bottom so save your wallet and leave those on the shelf. A brand called "Earthware" (look online) is reasonably priced and does a good job, or check stores like Walmart and Target for quality on a budget. Count on replacing pots and pans about once a year.

- A decent—meaning "sharp" set of knives in a knife block. Adding a sharpening stone is a plus (find at your local hardware store).

- Implements such as: spatulas, slotted spoons, tongs, scissors, wooden spoons, serving spoons, whisks, rubber spatulas—and something nice looking to keep them in next to the stove.

- A blender or food processor. If your place is in a tropical climate, a blender is a necessity. Your guests will want to make smoothies with the fresh fruit that's available, and of course, blender drinks for the drinkers in the group.

- Hand mixer.

- Mixing bowls.

- Measuring cups and spoons.

- Cutting boards. (These will save your countertops, although you may have to remind guests to use them.)

- Serving dishes, including platters.

- A serving tray.

- Placemats (something that can be wiped clean or washes easily).

- Pans for cooking in the oven—9-inch pyrex, broiler pan, meatloaf-size pan.

- Small containers for storing food.

- A pitcher.

Another of my pet peeves is chipped dishes and glasses. Try to get something that doesn't chip easily, and, especially if you have a pool and people will be drinking outdoors, decent PBA-free acrylic or plastic glasses are a great addition. These don't last forever—they tend to "craze"— so keep an eye out for end-of-season sales when you are in those discount stores.

You can determine how many place settings of dishes, set-ups of cutlery, and glasses your guests will need based on the number of people your house sleeps. It's always nice to have a couple of extras. That allows for renters to have guests over to eat, and for dishes to be in the dishwasher or waiting to be hand-washed and still have some available for use. Our house slept nine—so I had place settings for 12. Glasses are something you might as well stock up on. If you've got room to store them, have eight to 10 of each size (tall for cocktails, short for juice, and wine glasses for both red and white) for a house that sleeps six.

Cutlery and bowls tend to have a way of walking off, so you need to check every so often to make sure you've still got as much as you need. How do they walk off? Your guests may be vacationing with their friends down the street and they'll be sure to be sharing at least one meal together. They may decide to take a picnic meal to the beach, or to the dock at the lake. That's how your salad bowl ends up at your neighbor's rental—or in a trash can.

Renting Just a Room

- Small coffeemaker
- Small electric kettle
- Selection of decaf and caffeinated coffee
- Selection of teas
- Disposable coffee/tea cups
- A couple of spoons
- Small paper napkins
- A selection of packaged cookies or biscuits
- Small packets of sugar and creamer (dehydrated if necessary)

Even if you have a real B&B, try to set out an electric kettle or a Keurig (produces coffee and hot water for tea) cups or mugs, tea, instant coffee (there are some good ones now) or Keurig pods, dried cream, sugar and a few packaged biscuits in a common area. We stayed in a B&B in Rome one time in the summer and it was pretty warm so we'd do our touring in the mornings and return to the room for a little nap before we got ready to go out again for dinner. Although our host was lovely, she did not have any provisions available after breakfast, and one of her house rules was, "no food in the rooms." After our nap we would have loved a cup of tea or coffee and a cookie just to get us up and running again.

The Conundrum of Condiments

Guests will often ask if there are basic spices at the house or other condiments such as ketchup and mustard. In some climates, providing even salt and pepper can be a headache. Unless you keep salt in the fridge and put a generous amount of rice in the shaker, it is going to turn to stone if your home is anywhere near humidity.

Again, if you are the one doing the check-ins and check-outs, and you want to include basic condiments in your cost-of-doing-business, by all means, that will get you closer to being a "super-duper host." But if you are counting on a house manager who handles several other houses, you can't be assured that anything will be there when one set of guests leaves and another arrives. We had a grill that required charcoal and we did ask guests who used up the charcoal to buy some to leave for the next people, but that didn't always happen. I had to tell people they had better purchase coffee, salt and pepper, vegetable oil and any other condiments they wanted. When we were there, we'd check the casita and try to let upcoming guests know what was already there, but we still usually ended the season with a collection of small bottles of cooking oil, mustard, ketchup, and mayo.

* If you are renting a home that you live in part-time (or most of the time) the refrigerator should be emptied (*except for commonly-used condiments*) and washed out every time you are getting ready to receive new renters. Cupboards should also be emptied of perishables and washed out. You can leave standard spices, cooking oils, maybe vinegars, but anything else should be stored in your lock-up, given away or thrown out. Ditto for your liquor cabinet, unless it locks.

> *Anecdote: "You're taking Fiesta Ware to Mexico!"—said my friend, who also has a house in Mexico. She was mocking me out because Mexico has so much beautiful pottery and dinnerware. In her opinion, it was like taking coals to Newcastle, or—what would be today's equivalent of that expression??? Sand to the beach?*
>
> *Me: "Yes, it doesn't chip and the colors are perfect."* (*Keep in mind that countertops in Mexico are tile, cement, granite or marble. Knock over a long-stemmed wine glass or drop a cup and it's in two pieces for sure*). *I'm a big fan of Fiesta Ware so I have it in every kitchen. Twelve years into our rental we had lost a couple of cups and one small plate—and there weren't any chips to be found, except on the few Mexican serving dishes I had bought to add character.*
>
> *Oh—and remember the studio apartment in the Chateau outside of Paris that had been made into condos? The one*

where the owner walked through the fields dragging her suitcase to save taxi fare? The "small kitchen" consisted of a bar sink, a coffeemaker, a couple of dishes, a frying pan and a hot plate. Somehow my husband managed to cook several nice meals, including a delicious rabbit dinner for four people (we met new friends there) ... I still don't know how he did it.

Chapter 7

Build It, and They Will Come—The Pests, I Mean

"Pests" can mean anything from mosquitos, ants, bees, bedbugs, termites or scorpions, to mice, rats, even opossums. Although our worst fear was being stung by a scorpion, it was the other pests that became an integral part of our renting story.

The worst that ever happened to our renters were ant invasions and scorpion sightings, which was probably because when something weird involving animal or insect life happened to us, we solved the problem so it couldn't happen to guests. Fortunately, no one was ever stung at our home.

> *Anecdote: It had been kind of a crazy two weeks for us. We had just driven our Jeep (loaded up like the Beverly Hillbillies' flatbed trailer with totes full of dishes, sheets, a vacuum cleaner and various other paraphernalia we wanted for the new house) 3,600 miles from Buffalo to Sayulita. That was a six-day trip, made with a then six-year-old ginger tabby cat, Toto. During the trip, the A/C broke down so we drove the last 600 hot miles without it.*

> *When we arrived in Sayulita, we were a little stressed to say the least. The week of driving was followed with a week at a rental place, putting pressure on the builder to finish things and get the doors and windows in. He had told us the place would be livable before we left Buffalo a week earlier. The doors finally arrived and were installed, so we moved in. I looked at them and commented that it didn't look like they were quite finished, since there was a*

large gap at the tops. As it turned out I was right, the trim had yet to be installed.

We went to bed that night and both fell into a sound sleep until about 2 a.m., when I was awakened to the sound of cats wailing and Toto knocking over a lamp as he flew out the open window next to my head. I immediately thought about the five-foot gap between the house and the retaining wall behind it, and the fact we were two stories up. My mind was filled with the picture of poor Toto, lying smashed on the ground between the house and the wall.

I ran downstairs to open the doors so I could go out, and found the first floor alive with—feral cats. When they saw me, an intruder in a space where they had obviously been camping out every night, they scattered. One jumped straight up the eight-foot door and clung to the top where that gap was located. Another raced up the stairs. I followed that one, yelling at the slumbering Cal a cat was coming up. He didn't wake up until after the cat jumped on the bed and over his head on its way out the window on his side.

Finally, all of the cats were out of the house—but I still didn't know what had happened to Toto—until I looked out the window at the top of the stairs and saw him calmly sitting on the retaining wall, cleaning his paws. He had easily proven his physical prowess to us by jumping the gap; and his alpha-ness to the feral cats, by clearing them out of what was now his domain.

But I Digress—Let's Talk About Pests

Chances are, the space you are renting out is either in the tropics, or you are renting most during the summer months, when any kind of special "guest" might be likely to show up. Bugs are part of summer life—and they are also part of life in the tropics, but on a grander scale. Guests do not appreciate bugs of any description, and they will hold you responsible if there's an infestation, whether it was within your control or not.

I know the trend is to use natural insect repellents and certainly, that is the preferred method. If, however, you live in the southern or southwestern U.S., or the vacation home you are renting is in the tropics, it's unlikely that spraying Neem, salt spray; mineral oil; citrus oil and cayenne pepper; soap, orange citrus oil and water; eucalyptus oil; onion and garlic oil or chrysanthemum flower tea is going to have much of an effect on fire ants, cutter ants or … scorpions.

There are a lot of natural-based insect repellants listed on the web, and you might want to try them out before you go to the hard, not-environmentally-friendly stuff. Trial and error will tell you what works. If the natural cures aren't working, you may have to go for the chemicals, sorry. But the alternative, having your guest bitten by an invasion of fire ants or a scorpion (we never had a guest bitten by a scorpion), is not fun and will NOT result in a good review.

Most scorpion bites are not lethal, but they are very uncomfortable and typically require a shot of anti-venom. Those who are allergic to scorpion bites can go into anaphylactic shock, which could result in death—not that I'm trying to scare you.

Anecdote: We did have few uncomfortable encounters with scorpions. Once, we were watching a movie in bed and one dropped from the ceiling to the bed right between us. It made a bee-line (or scorpion-line) under the covers at the foot of the bed, but Cal knocked it off with his shoe and squashed it. Scorpions don't usually make an appearance unless their homes have been disturbed, and we had just had a rainstorm that brought down a sizable chunk of the adjacent hill.

Then there was the time some enterprising soul burned off the brush at the top of the hill and the housekeeper swept up 17 of them in the second bedroom ... The Momma scorpion the gardener found. She had 20 babies on her back. Scorpions are very creepy-looking, but they aren't all that quick, so if you keep your eyes peeled, you are likely to see them before they sting you. They do like to hide under things, however, which is why it's important to emphasis to guests that they shouldn't leave towels or clothes on the floor.

You may have to retain an exterminator to come on a regular basis to do major control around your unit. New York City, Florida and the Southern U.S., are notorious for cockroaches. We've already discussed bedbugs, which are common in any area where there's a lot of travelers. And in the tropics, palapa roofs are practically pest hotels. These are the very lovely, romantic-looking shelters made from palm leaves that are traditional in tropical areas—but they are also home to insects of all types, plus mice, lizards ... sometimes even snakes.

You will need to keep a large spray bottle of strong insecticide around because in the tropics and pretty much any vacation home when the ants come marching—and they will come marching—it can be overwhelming. You never know when the little dudes are going to show up.

We had two invasions of fire ants, one not half an hour before new guests were to arrive for the casita, and one up behind our second bedroom where we housed family and friends (and the occasional people we had double-booked). My husband happened to go out one night to check on a light and walked right into a blanket of them covering the entire path at the back of the building—in his sandals. Ouch!

Cutter ants are also fairly common in the tropics and are fascinating to watch. They carry pieces of leaves that are at least three times their body size from the plant to their nest and use the leaves to grow mold, which they then eat. They can strip a bougainvillea within a day, however, so even though we loved watching them, we had to spray them to save our beautiful bushes.

Being reasonably clean and tidy helps prevent unwanted invasions of insects. Many houses in the tropics are open to the elements because basically, when we're escaping a cold winter to someplace warm and sunny, we want to feel like we're living outdoors. This makes it impossible to screen off every entry. So here's a few hints:

- Instruct guests NOT to leave clothing or towels lying on the floor. Scorpions, as I said, like to be under things and the more things you leave for them to be under, the more likely you'll encounter one. (Just an aside—cats are actually faster than scorpions and will kill them, so if you take your cat to the tropics like we did, you don't have to worry about it dying of a scorpion bite.)

- If it is warm, there will be flies. And if you do not control your food garbage, there will be maggots. I found keeping a small compost container lined with a plastic bag next to the sink for food scraps, then tying up the small bag when it was full before putting it in a larger garbage bag helped a lot. This meant everything was double-wrapped, which can mean extra plastic, but you can get the bio-degradable plastic bags. It's worth it.

- Check, or have your house manager check, for wasp or bees nests under the eaves or outdoor furnishings.

- Food should not be left out. It will attract ants, guaranteed. In one of the upscale resorts close to us on the West Coast of Mexico, all of the rooms were palapa cottages, with kitchens and living spaces open to the tropical breezes. Guests were warned not to leave food out because they might be visited at night by a tejon, a type of a badger which likes to snack on human food. What the heck—it's easier than scrounging around for food in the jungle.

- Keep trees trimmed and away from the roof of your house. Animals climb trees and travel from the tree to the roof, and possibly onto your terrace and into your house. They are wild. Even the cats you may encounter are probably feral. They are not nice kitty cats, and will be aggressive when approached by human beings. Don't feed them either. If they get used to finding food when you are there, what will they do when you are not there?

If you don't have screens everywhere, mosquitos and no-see-'ems are likely to be a problem at dusk or after dusk. Again, essential oils might work for some people: citronella, clove, lemongrass, rosemary, tea tree, cajeput, eucalyptus, cedar, catnip, geranium, lavender and mint are popular ingredients. You might want to remind guests to bring the bug repellant of their choice with them. We always kept a basket of sunscreens, bug repellant, aloe and after-bite in a basket next to the main door, where it was handy. This worked well as when guests left, they'd often leave their leftovers in the basket rather than carry them home on the plane.

Mosquito nets are useful in bedrooms that aren't completely screened in, plus they do add to the ambience. There is also a product called "Bug Off" screens available online that temporarily fix to doorways and windows using tension rods. These can be useful. They are advertised specifically for people with pets who like to go in and out at will, but they work well for people too and they do keep the majority of flying insects outside instead of inside.

Anecdote: What to choose? The iguana in the kitchen sink? The day a friend and I sat wondering why there were so many pieces of dead bees under the floor fan —until the bee-sting covered house manager from next door came over to tell us to lock up the house and leave while the exterminators removed the huge beehive next door. There are so many stories to tell, but I think this one is the best:

As I explained earlier, every year we traveled to our house in Mexico, we took our cat, Toto, in the car the two times that we drove, and by plane the many years we flew. Toto hated flying but he loved Sayulita because it was warm and it was pretty much outdoor living. Even at night he could go out on the terrace outside the master bedroom and sleep under the stars. One night, I awoke to the sound of his hissing at something. Instantly alert, I jumped out of bed and turned on the lights to the terrace—but saw nothing that he could be hissing at. Toto, in the meantime, had ambled off downstairs to sleep on the couch.

Since I was up, I thought I might as well make a visit to the bathroom. I was sitting on the throne in the little toilet room, with the door open because my husband was sound asleep, when I spied what looked like a small foot poking out underneath the door. I'm blind as a bat without my glasses, so I thought maybe my eyes were playing tricks on me. I pushed on the door. It pushed back. Now, I was about five feet from the bed, but somehow I manage to leap from the toilet to the bed without touching the floor. (This might be too much information, but let me just say, I wasn't quite finished what I was doing ...)

My scream woke my husband, "Snake! Iguana! Something is in the bathroom!" He got up, blurry-eyed and reached for the flashlight he kept in his bedside table, telling me to go downstairs to find something he could use as a weapon. When I returned with the broom and dustpan (What help was that going to be, he asked?), he was staring into the bathroom at the bright little eyes of a possum that was now hiding behind the toilet. He stood back and wistfully said, "Now how am I going to get that out of there?"

With his usual pragmatism, Cal decided that whatever he was going to do, it could wait until morning. He reached in and opened the bathroom window, then shut the door and went back to bed. I also went back to bed, but abandoned trying to sleep there as I could hear the little critter scratching at the door and walls. I went downstairs to sleep on the couch with Toto.

Next morning, when I took Cal his coffee, the first order of the day was, "What do we do about the possum?" Before we headed to the animal shelter to borrow a Have-a-Heart trap, we opened the bathroom door, and—miraculously, since we were two stories up—the possum had gone out the window. We think he landed on the small roof just below the window (that covered the hot water tank) and was able to safely make it to the ground from there. From that day forward, we made sure no tree branches came close enough to the house for an animal to climb across to the roof. Plus, I stopped leaving cat food out on the terrace. Cal rolling his eyes here ...

And then there's this one—which didn't have such a happy ending:

One year, my two daughters were staying with us, occupying the second bedroom. There was a door at the top of the stairs that lead outside to a short bridge and at the end of the bridge was the door going into the second bedroom. One night my oldest, Nathalie, said goodnight to us and was off up the stairs to go to bed. We heard her open the door at the top of the stairs, then heard it quickly slam shut, accompanied by a scream. (It would have to be Nathalie, the most dramatic of my offspring.)

Me: "What's wrong?"

Nathalie: "There's a strange animal out there staring at me!"

Me: "What does it look like?"

Nathalie: "Half dog, half rat."

Me (now experienced in the local animal husbandry): "Oh, it's a possum."

There were a few jokes and laughter, and Cal had to grab the broom (our weapon of choice, remember) to go out and keep the possum away from the girls (I'm calling them girls but they were both over 35 at the time) so they could get from the main house to the second bedroom without being attacked by this "vicious" possum. The next morning, they complained they had heard it moving around and making noises all night. I assured them the possum was more afraid of them than vice versa, but my assurances fell on deaf ears.

The next night we all joked about what the excitement would be when Nathalie and Blythe went to bed, but Cal and I were certain the possum would be gone and all would be well. Nathalie went up the stairs. Door opens, door quickly slams shut again.

"It's there!" she said. And we do a repeat performance of the night before. The following day, Cal decides the problem is serious enough to call an exterminator, who comes with a Have-a-Heart trap. When they return for the trap a day later, the possum is in residence, so they take her (I will explain how we know it was a "she.") away and relocate her where she can't scare grown women out of their wits when the two come face-to-face.

About a week later, we begin to smell this really, really bad odor between the two buildings, around the bridge. It didn't take me long (It's amazing how life offers up valuable experiences with mice and other small creatures.), to figure out this smell is something dead. A little investigation leads us to deduce that the possum was a mother, who had placed her babies inside an uncovered drain pipe going from the bridge down to the garden. Without their mom, the babies had starved to death in the drain pipe and we were horrible, possum-baby murderers of the worst kind.

As badly as we felt about the babies, it was almost impossible to flush their bodies out of the pipe and get rid of the smell. It took days of hosing and finally some muriatic acid and a power washer to dislodge them. Then we had to call the ironworker to build a grate to put over the opening to the pipe so this could not happen again. All in all, not an inexpensive episode in our litany of pest problems. And to this day, I feel guilty when I think of those baby possums!

Coffee bar on the terrace where the first possum made its appearance. "Staged" for the photo with the FiestaWare coffee mug and a book. Great place to spend the first hour of the day!

Chapter 8

Make Your "Renters Book" a Best Seller

What is a "Renters Book?" Many rentals don't actually have a book—they may have a page of minimal instructions on the Ins and Outs of your stay—and that might be enough if you are renting a single room. But if you are renting an apartment or a whole house, it's probably not sufficient. We all become used to our own spaces, so we don't think about the fact that some locks are tricky, microwaves all run differently, and even toilets have their own eccentricities. Those are the things you need to think about when you put together a list of instructions and house rules for your rental. The phrase "never assume" should be the rule of thumb as to what to put into the Renters Book.

Renters are also appreciative if you give them the "native's tour" of the area. What should they see, what restaurants are best and what should they watch out for?

First, What Should the "Renters Book" Look Like?

The basic rules of graphic design apply here because— people don't like to read a lot of text (repeat, repeat, repeat):

- Put a photo of the house/building on the cover. You can use a three-ring binder, and many of these have a clear-plastic slot you can easily slip the photo/cover page into. It doesn't have to be professionally printed. You may have to update the book regularly, so just use plain paper and print off of your printer (in color, preferably).

- Use clear plastic sleeves to insert the pages. This protects them and also gives you the option to change them individually when you need to update.

- Break up the information into short, concise paragraphs.

- Don't single space—at the minimum, set the spacing to 1.2, and don't use a fancy font, or anything smaller than 12 pts. If your market is retirees, like me, they can't read the small print. And even younger folks like their reading on the easy side.

- Use lots of bullet-pointed lists.

- Use headlines and sub-heads.

- Feel free to use color for the text, as long as it's easy to read.

- And put in pictures—lots of pictures (more on those later).

Next, What to Say in the Renters Book

You want renters to respect your property, so you might want to start with an introduction as to who you are and what the place means to you (above and beyond its rental income potential, for example: "Casa Viliano is our home. We live here four months out of the year ... blah, blah, blah."). Your cover photo could include a picture of you (and your spouse/partner, if there is one). The more you personalize your rental space, the better people are going to treat it. They will regard it as your home or a space you've worked hard to make nice for them, and people are more respectful of things that belong to their "friends" than they are of things belonging to complete strangers.

Those Disappearing Pictures

Go around the house/apartment and take photos of any of the art, plants, gardens, decorations, etc. you have that look appealing. You can use these, plus some of the photos you've used on the web page to break up your text. The pictures in the book also create a record of what you have in the house and where it is located, just in case something disappears or gets moved. One friend who rented her house in Sayulita found her small original paintings consistently disappeared from the walls. They were easy to pack, I guess.

Break Up the Text

- Housekeeping—What do you do with garbage? If there are services such as maid, gardener, or pool guy, when should the guests expect them to come? If you provide breakfast, what time? How do the microwave, stove and oven work? Is there laundry in the unit, or where they can take their laundry? Can you run the toaster and the microwave together or will the circuit breaker blow? When and who do they call if they have a problem?

- Medical care—what do they do if someone has an accident that the first aid kits in your bathrooms won't cover? Give a list of reliable doctors, clinics or hospitals and include their locations and phone numbers. Give the number for an ambulance. This requires some research, and typically the neighbors or the ex-pat community will be able to help you collect the best information you can provide.

- Money—Which ATMs should they use? Is it safe to carry a substantial amount of cash? Do you have safes in your units? (See Appendix 1)

- Groceries—Where can they buy produce, staples? Is there a local market that's good and fun to go to?

- Local restaurants—Which ones do you recommend? What are the price ranges? Are they appropriate for small children?

- House manager—How should they contact the house manager? When should they contact the house manager?

- WiFi—What's the password and user name?

- Where can they find a spare light bulb if one burns out?

- Locking up instructions. You or the house manager will show people how to lock up when you check them in, but they might be tired from traveling or excited about having arrived, and they may miss some of the instructions. Put them in the book on a separate page for quick reference.

- Tours—Are there sight-seeing tours; hiking; biking; sailing; deep-sea fishing? What are the best ones to do and the best places to sign up? Can they get a special price by mentioning they are staying at your place?

- A local map is helpful, if you can find one.

- House rules (more on those in the next chapter).

In addition to the lengthier text inside the book, I also recommend a "Cliff's Notes" page with just the essentials, either on one of the covers or as the first insert. This is for the people who don't have the patience to read through the book, although if the book is attractive, entertaining and useful information, most people will read it.

As I said, don't assume everyone knows how to run everything you own. Not all appliances are the same. Even coffeemakers can be quite different—some people may not have experience with a French press or an espresso percolator. If you have a coffee maker that's different from what most folks have (In the U.S. we mainly have drip coffee pots or Keurigs.), leave instructions.

Light switches can also be a challenge for those who don't know your house. We ended up labeling ours so there was no question which one to use.

Anecdote: While we were interviewing architects and contractors to build our house in Mexico, we stayed in the second-floor apartment of "Casa Juanita" with our delightful host, "Tuck" living just below on the first floor. One evening, Cal decided to put something in the oven for dinner. All the stoves in Mexican pueblos run on propane and some of the small ones—like the one Cal was working with—don't have automatic ignition and have to be lit with a match.

When he turned on the gas and bent over to light the pilot, there was a loud explosion. The lids on two pots he was using on top of the stove flew off, and Cal's legs were rendered hairless—even his eyebrows were singed. Tuck came flying up the stairs to see what had happened and told us that in the five years she had owned the place, the oven had never been used. You never know what guests will take it into their heads to use, so it's probably a good idea to test drive every appliance once in awhile and make sure you leave instructions for use—just to make sure there's no surprises.

Some photos of the pictures and knick-knacks that make your place look homey, but might be inclined to disappear into a renters' suitcase will dress up your Renters Book while documenting what you have in your house. This can help prevent those things from disappearing.

Chapter 9

Rules, Regulations and Agreements

Most web sites now have a section for "house rules," but you can be pretty sure the renters inquiring about your space are not going to read through those, other than to check to see if you allow smoking and pets. Try to keep the house rules to a minimum—people are coming to your place to have fun, after all—but also try to find ways to repeat the important rules so they are actually imprinted on your renters' brains.

In small-town Mexico, for example in many homes you cannot put toilet paper in the toilet—AT ALL (this means feminine hygiene products are also excluded from being flushed). As a host, I listed this in the Renters Book, in the Cliff notes, verbally told renters at check-in, and had signs next to the toilets. Out of habit, even I made the mistake of putting the occasional wad of paper in the toilet, but with all the reminders around, most people caught on pretty quickly.

You also should not use produce (fruits or vegetables) in Mexico without first soaking it in Micodyne or Bacdyne, which they sell in the grocery stores. I left this out next to the kitchen sinks, in addition to mentioning it in the book and on a counter sign. Soaking fruits and veggies meant the difference between staying healthy and getting Montezuma's revenge, so it's kind of an important rule in countries where the irrigation water is not necessarily clean.

Some other things you might want to control:

- Smoking—smoking disturbs non-smoking guests, so you definitely don't want to allow it inside your home, but you also might need to specify where people should go to smoke outdoors so the smoke doesn't blow into a unit that's occupied by someone else.

- Pets—need to be quiet and well-behaved, which means the owners have to have control over them. Dogs should be walked regularly so they don't have to do their business in the unit or close to it. Similar to smokers, you might want to suggest where a dog can be walked, and provide plastic bags to be used to pick up after them.

- Noise—set hours for the time noise has to be turned down, and (especially if you live in a neighborhood) tell your guests that this rule MUST be obeyed.

- Housecleaning—note whether or not cleaning is included in the rental fee, or if there's an extra charge. Sometimes guests will offer to clean themselves in order to save some money. That's your decision. Our house was large, with probably 3,000 square feet of tile floors—I couldn't clean them myself, and labor in developing countries is relatively cheap—so there was no point in giving people money off the price to clean the house themselves. I just told guests that wasn't an option. I did ask that guests do their own dishes. The maid didn't have time to wash a load of dishes either during her mid-week cleaning or after the guests left.

I have stayed at houses where we've been asked to strip the beds, start the laundry, and sweep all of the floors before we left. Most guests won't mind doing minimal chores like that. We always left a broom and dustpan handy, so people could clean up if they felt they needed to. Disinfectant wipes are also a handy thing to leave out, especially if someone happened to get sick.

Renters might glance through the "house rules" noted on the web, but if you really want to enforce your rules, you'll find you have to repeat them at check-in and/or in your Renters Book. Even if your guests have read your rules online, they might be arriving months after they read them and they'll have forgotten. If you establish your expectations from the start of the visit, there won't be any question of what's appropriate and what's not.

Anecdote: One thing we did not anticipate having to include in our house rules, was a statement about clothes—whether you had to wear them or not. It just didn't occur to us, and we were about 10 years into renting before this became an issue. We took a booking for the casita from a lovely middle-aged couple who had their own B&B in central British Columbia. They were able to travel during the winter, because summertime was their high season.

Matt and Jane had just settled into the casita, when Matt came up and asked Cal if it was okay if Jane went topless at the pool. Their place, which also had a pool, was "clothing optional," and they advertised it accordingly, he told Cal. I was sitting at my desk, within hearing distance, when the question was posed. Now, if they had been one of the twenty-something, very buff couples that we frequently hosted, my input might have been a little different. They were, however, middle-aged, with bodies that (like ours), were showing the effects of gravity.

We aren't prudes, we did skinny dip in our pool after dark—but even though the pool was reasonably secluded—we didn't do it in the daytime.

I looked at Cal and said, "Well, it's not going to bother me, if it doesn't bother you."

He kind of grinned and said, "Sure!"

The pool and the pool deck were right outside our living room and kitty-corner to a terrace off of the living room, where we hung out quite a bit. It took us about two days to get used to seeing Matt and Jane sunbathing on the pool deck, completely sin ropas—*as they say in Mexico. After that two days, we had to acknowledge that nudity is not really such a big thing. We didn't notice bodies, we just saw people, people we talked with and began to consider friends.*

Jane, who is British, actually has beautiful skin, and I asked her one day what her dermatologist thought about the amount of sunbathing she did. "I don't have one," she replied. At that moment I kind of wished I didn't either. I diligently apply 50+ sunscreen and sit in the shade all the time, but even that's not enough for my skin-Nazi. She would only be happy if all I ever wore was a burqa.

Rental Agreements—What You Should Include

A rental agreement protects you and your renters. There's plenty of samples online, plus, as I said, one in the appendix of this book. You can adapt a sample format to your specific needs. Basically, the rental agreement should cover:

- The amount of the rental fee, any additional fees (such as cleaning, damage deposit or city tax), and the said total fees.

- The amount of the deposit, the date the deposit is due, and the date the remainder is due.

- Your cancellation policy.

- Your policy regarding the damage deposit: What will you charge people for? When do you want to be notified there has been damage? When will you return the damage deposit?

- What time is check in? What time is check out?

- What is your policy regarding: use of the laundry; lost keys; the swimming pool; any recreational vehicles you are including in the rental?

- What is your policy if the renters experience a theft while they are staying at your place?

- What are the house rules?

- Use of a safe?

What is your liability, should a renter be injured at your home? This will depend on what country you are renting from and liability is very different in Mexico, for example, than it is in the U.S. If possible, you should carry a fairly hefty liability insurance policy just in case someone is seriously injured at your rental. This can be tricky if your rental home is in a foreign country, so it may require some research.

A Touchy Topic: Security

In first world countries, things get stolen, but people who are vacationing in second or third world countries have a way of forgetting that. Bicycles that are not locked up disappear, wallets are taken, purses are grabbed, cars are broken into for small change—cars are stolen, in fact. When people go on vacation in a second- or third-world country and they experience a theft, all of a sudden, the house they are staying in is not safe. They get pick-pocketed, and the buses, or the subways, or the country they are visiting itself is not safe.

Sorry folks, the problem—as most travel writers will say—is not your environment, it is you. People on vacation are not in the same mindset as they are when they are home. They are excited. They've saved up to pay for this vacation, they are in a different culture, they're treating themselves to luxuries they don't usually have, or maybe they're in town for a destination wedding, and they are usually drinking more alcohol than they usually drink. For these reasons, they do things they wouldn't normally do, the primary thing being: not locking up.

Renters want safes, and they think if they put their money and valuables in a safe, it is safe. Not true. Thieves—who are likely watching rental properties looking for an opportunity to get into a house—know that the first place to look for money is the safe. If you were a thief, wouldn't it be in your best interest to know how to get into safes, since that's where the cash is? Certain safe companies only have 50 different locks for the hundreds of thousands of safes that they sell, and even combination safes have back-up keys. If thieves can get their hands on 10 keys for those safes, they have a one in five chance of opening the safe in your unit. The safe companies themselves say (in the small print) that a safe is only one factor in keeping your money and valuables out of the hands of thieves.

A theft will almost always result in a bad review, even if you reimburse the renters for the theft. It may result in the return of rental monies, because the renter moves out of your unit earlier than planned. Here are some tips for keeping thefts to a minimum:

- Tell renters: lock up; lock up; lock up! Make sure they understand how to lock all doors and windows and that they need to do it every time they leave the property, and at night before bed.

- Suggest they don't keep large amounts of money on them or in the safe. In our experience, most small-town robbers are looking only for money. They don't want items they have to fence that might be found in their possession or traced back to them. It is more expensive, obviously, to make several small withdrawals at an ATM than one large one, but it's still cheaper than losing a few hundred dollars.

- There are times and locations where it's better to have a unique hiding place rather than a safe. You can purchase many different forms of containers to hold money—shaving gel cans, peanut butter jars and travel coffee mugs. Guests can buy their own and bring them in their suitcase. I guess I wouldn't choose a soda pop can, because a thief might just think he needs a refreshment while he's at your place.

- ATMs can also be compromised. We learned this the hard way when our bank account was drained of $6,000 over a weekend while we were in

Mexico—by a mob from the Ukraine. The bank reimbursed us, but we are all paying for these incidents through interest rates and bank fees. Suggest that guests have a separate checking account to use when they are traveling and only keep $500 or so in it. Another option is a pre-paid debit card that can be replenished when it runs out. If you know which ATMs are safest in your community, recommend those to your renters.

- One of the rules in the Renters Book should be: "Do not invite people you have just met up to the house/unit." New "friends" may just be scoping out the place for their pals, the professional burglars.

- Pick-pockets are a problem, particularly in larger cities. Travelers should carry their money in secure purses, pouches or backpacks, and they should be careful about putting those items down for ANY reason. A friend of ours put his backpack down to pick something up for an old lady in Mexico City, and the backpack was gone when he stood up. So now our inside joke is: "If someone throws a baby at you when you have your backpack in your hand, DON'T put down your backpack to catch the baby!"

There were several occasions when we did reimburse people for thefts if we thought they had really been careful with where they put money that was taken. It's your decision whether you're going to do that or not. The question is always: was the loss the result of poor security in the unit, or was it due to carelessness on the part of the renter? There's an article about money safety that I send to renters in the Appendix 1 of this book.

Anecdote: We mainly reimbursed people for smaller thefts when we thought the security at our house was somehow lacking. Once, two young men were staying in our casita and through our emails, I came to believe they were very careful individuals. They had not had a vacation in five years because they hadn't been able to afford to travel. In the middle of their stay, I got a desperate phone call. They had put money in their bedside table (NOT a safe place), locked up the casita and left. When they returned, the money (about $300) was gone and they needed it for the remainder of their trip. They were going to Mexico City the next day.

As I said, I thought they seemed pretty reliable and I also believed they did not have a lot of money, so I refunded the $300 even though they had left the money right where we told them not to—in the bedside table. The house manager later informed me they had left the kitchen window wide open—which was the equivalent of inviting the thieves inside. Another upshot of this was the upstairs renters, who at first said the second bedroom had been broken into but they had not lost anything, suddenly found they were also short $300. I had to reimburse them, too, of course.

In another incident, a group of vacationers arrived in our little town at a rental unit right on the beach early in the afternoon. The house manager gave them instructions on locking up when they were checked in. The group was so excited to have reached their destination that they grabbed swimsuits and immediately ran out to jump in the ocean—without locking the house. When they returned, everything of value was gone, money, computers, phones, cameras.

Chapter 10

Securing Your Own "Stuff"

If you live in your rental unit part of the time, you'll want to have a closet or cupboard somewhere in the place where you can easily store all of your personal things and LOCK UP. When your home is being rented, it should look pretty much like a hotel room, with some exceptions. Most renters don't want to see your clothes in the closet, personal items in the bathrooms, or even your family photos sitting out. They may, however, not mind seeing or drinking your fine tequila.

Out of necessity, home-sharing has evolved somewhat in regard to leaving your personal belongings. If you only rent the place occasionally and for a few days at a time, it is permissible to leave some closets and drawers with clothes in them and some of your personal items out in the open. Cal and I rented an apartment in Milan for just two nights and the woman left most of her clothing, shoes and beauty products in the walk-in closet. Everything was organized and beautifully displayed, however, right down to the dozen shades of nail polish on the bathroom shelf. There weren't any dirty toothbrushes or smelly sweat pants to be seen. It was like browsing through a small boutique.

The rule of thumb should be: If you don't want anyone touching something that belongs to you, put it away in a locked space. Simple locks don't always keep people out, so you will want to make sure your "lock-up closet" is really secure. People are strange—they love to explore other people's things.

There are several options for storing clothing, but where your home is located will influence which option you choose. If the area is high humidity, it can be a challenge to store clothes and not have them come out smelling musty, or even actually sporting mildew. Here's a few tips:

- Launder EVERYTHING right before you put it away. Skin oils attract insects and any soil has the potential to turn into a petri dish on your favorite shirt.

- Look online for clothing storage bags. There are space bags (vacuum seal so when you suck the air out, the package also gets smaller), grey bags (reported to be the best for repelling humidity), boxes and totes. Choose something recommended for your climate. If you do have humidity, you'll also want to use a desiccant, which is a chemical substance that absorbs moisture. Various forms of desiccants are available online. Sachets or dryer sheets will also help repel bugs and add some nice fragrance, but don't put dryer sheets right next to fabric. I learned from experience they can leave a yellow stain.

- Totes work well for knick-knacks, dishes, photos, everything else that you don't want to leave out— and they are reusable. Careful what size you use and how you pack them, they can get really heavy.

- Package shoes separately.

- Purchase the desiccants that come in bags to hang up in your closet—use them as a double-precaution against mildew.

Packing and unpacking is a chore—there's no getting around it. It's pretty much the same as moving, and we all know moving ranks right up there with divorce and a death in the family as far as stress is concerned. The one good thing about packing up the personal things in your rental home is that when you unpack them, it's kind of like Christmas or a birthday. You'll be delighted to find things you've forgotten you even had!

Security or "Candid" Cameras

Outdoor security cameras are one way to help make your property safer, but they do have their limitations. Good thieves know how to disguise themselves with hoodies, throw things over the camera, unscrew lights, and sometimes even steal the cameras themselves. If your area is subject to thefts (not too many resort areas don't have some level of crime) and you can have a security camera installed in an obscure place that's hard to reach and have it connect to the local police, it's probably worth the investment.

Installing a camera inside your unit for the purpose of watching your guests is a much more controversial topic. Personally, I think it's a total invasion of privacy—much worse than going in and leaving post-it notes all over—as one of our hosts did.

If you follow these suggestions:

- Develop a rapport with your renters by email.

- Charge an equitable fee for your place (not pricing it as though it were a hostel).

- Either you or your house manager meet the guests at check-in.

- And you have stated the house rules on the website, in the renter's agreement and in your Renters Book, then you should have established the level of behavior and respect for your property that you are expecting from your guests.

You can also Google prospective renters to get some idea of their background, plus, some of the home-sharing rental sites include background information on guests and reviews of the guests.

Of course, you can take all of these steps and still have a problem once in awhile. We had a youngish couple in our casita one time who left it filthy (popcorn and sand all over), and somehow had managed to soak every towel and every rug, all of which they left on the floor. The rugs smelled so bad our housecleaner daintily picked them up in two fingers and put them right into the washer. Nothing was permanently damaged, but it's never a good feeling to have someone treat your property badly.

Occasional breakages, loss of flashlights, cutlery, dishes and even small pictures are all part of the cost of doing business. If you have significant damages, report them to the listing web site immediately and make a claim. That is the entire purpose of charging a security deposit.

My rule of thumb is to treat renters the way I like to be treated, and being caught on "candid camera" is not something I'd appreciate. If you feel you need to install interior cameras to see what's going on in your house when it has been rented, then maybe you should reconsider the home-sharing business.

Anecdotes: Renters are people, and people are people, they all seem to be curious about other people's stuff, so if it's not locked up properly, hmmm …

There was the year we left Cal's special anejo tequila on the top shelf of the lock-up closet. We had traveled to the town of Tequila (a five-hour drive) and purchased a liter jug of the anejo at a special distillery our friends had told us about. This tequila was a particularly delicious, smooth, vanilla-y sipping tequila. We trustingly left it high up on the very back of the shelf. There wasn't a drop left when we returned. The culprits turned out to be renters who told us they had pried open the closet so they could "hide" their camera in it.

If You're Renting, Why Not Also List on a Home-Exchange Site

Like many other homeowners who rent their places on home-sharing web sites, we thought exchanging our house for someplace in an exotic local would be a great, economical idea, so we tried it a few times. From my point of view, the same standards that applied to renting applied to home exchanges. We provided our home exchange customers exactly the same level of service as our paying customers, and we expected a somewhat comparable situation in return. The problem with home exchanges is that many of the homes listed are not rented out, so they are not set up with check-in or cleaning services. Nor are the homeowners geared to clearing out their space for strangers.

The year we visited a home exchange in the highlands of Scotland heralded the end of our home exchanges. We had housed a family of seven at our house for two weeks, providing a "hotel-ready" environment when they arrived, twice-weekly maid service at no charge, and air-conditioning in the master bedroom and the casita. When the two of us arrived at their "romantic" Scottish cottage, the owners' used toothbrushes were sitting next to the sink in the bathroom and the closets were jammed with rather smelly clothing.

There was a washing machine, but no dryer. Although it was June, the weather was cold and rainy the whole two-and a half-weeks that we stayed, so we couldn't dry clothes outside. The entire time we were "at home" we lived in the living room surrounded by laundry because there was a fireplace to keep us warm and to actually dry the clothes. I went to change the sheets on the bed after a week and couldn't find another set that wasn't ripped or stained. Oh—and we paid a cleaning fee to have the place cleaned after we left.

The weather wasn't the owner's fault, but when it comes to home exchanges, some effort should be made to equalize the value of the two experiences. And at the very least, no dirty toothbrushes in cups, please!

Chapter 11

The Question of What to Charge

Now that you've gone to a lot of work making your place look great and feel great for guests, you probably think your first idea about pricing was low end. There's only one way to find out and it's going to take time: research. Go to the home-sharing websites, do a search for a place similar to yours—one room, one bedroom, two-bedroom—and see what they are charging. Here's what you want to look for:

- Location: Where is your home located with respect to popular tourist attractions, public transportation, the beach, a lake, grocery stores, and shopping? Is there anything on your street (which renters will pass by either driving or walking) that would detract from the location? Do you have views and what views will people see from your house?

- Amenities: What does your place offer compared to others in the price range you're thinking about? Do you offer television/cable, WiFi, well-equipped kitchen, barbecue, on-site laundry, beach towels, beach chairs and umbrellas, kayaks, canoes, bicycles, pool, hot tub?

- Is cleaning included in your price? How frequently?

- How many people does your house sleep?

It's also a good idea to look at places that are not "comparable" to yours, look at the lower end such as hostels, and the higher-end. This will confirm the appropriate price for your unit. As you gather this information, it's useful to put it into a grid or table of some sort. List about four or five places that are similar to yours, and what they charge by night and by the week. Do they give a discount for a week or longer?

You don't need to put the low-end or high-end places in your grid, but at least you have a mental picture of what is being offered in these ranges. Our casita, for example, was a small studio, but it did have a large, private terrace and many amenities you couldn't get in a hostel. When you get inquiries, some people will want to negotiate a lower price. Knowing that the hostels in our area charged $50/night told me our place was worth more, and helped me stick to my guns. We were about a 10-minute walk to the beach, so I also knew I couldn't charge as much as a house on the beach or one block from the beach.

Circumstances such as the street that led up to our house (as I mentioned, it was a very poor Mexican neighborhood) do affect how your place compares with others. We always priced our place accordingly, and remember, I always told people who were thinking about renting about the road, so they wouldn't be surprised when they got there.

By looking at your grid, you should get a pretty good idea of what to charge. People do not like add-on charges, such as cleaning or air conditioning or charges for pets. My own personal preference is to include the cost of these services in your nightly and weekly rates, but that is really up to you. There were times when we probably should have added a pet fee, like when the dog peed all over the plastic rug and we had to throw it out, but overall, we didn't have a lot of problems with pets.

If your rental unit is in a location that has a high season, low season, and Holiday season, you will need to figure out different price levels. Again, look at what your competition is charging and charge accordingly. We were able to add about $400 a week to our high season price during the Holidays, a friend who had a condo on the beach doubled her high season price for the Holidays—it's whatever the market will bear.

Know that it is going to take some time to build your business, but don't start drastically discounting rates to get started. Most renters will relate the price they are paying to how much respect they show for your property and the things you have in it. If we had priced the casita at the same rate as the hostels, we would not have attracted the quality renters we did, and we would have had more damages and more maintenance. Also, if you charge too little, potential guests tend to think there's something wrong with your place. If your unit is priced fairly or maybe even slightly above market rate and looks good in the photos, it will rent, you'll get good renters and good reviews and your business will build.

Once you've built a reputation, you might expect your rental to book up at least a year in advance. Not every place will work that way. If yours is a popular location for Christmas and New Year's (it's near a ski resort or is in a warm weather spot), then you will probably book those seasons well in advance. If yours is a place that's popular for Holidays like Presidents Week or Easter, you'll have some folks thinking ahead. However, if you're in a sunny climate in the South or south of the border, you might not book up until the weather in the North gets bad and people start thinking about making a getaway to get some relief. We got to be pretty confident our casita would rent from December to June, so we didn't give discounts to people who inquired early and asked for money off.

You can give 10 percent or 15 percent for people who book a week or more, but when they start asking for a steep discount because they want to stay a month—think about it. It's more wear and tear on your property because they won't eat out or go out as much, and—if you know your place will rent three weeks out of a month for sure, don't go lower than what it would be for those three weeks.

If you have listed your unit on more than one website, check to make sure your rates are quoted the same on every site. It can get a little confusing because you may have high season, low season, and Holiday rates, plus you'll have to state if you give a discount for a week or longer. On some sites you'll have to designate the dates these rates change. Nowadays, prospective renters look at more than one site and believe me, they'll check to make sure they are getting the cheapest rate possible. If your rates and dates they change are not listed as the same amount across the board, you'll end up charging them the lowest rate they see.

There'll be times you are on the other side of this business equation—you're looking to book the best spot for your family get-together during the Holidays, or for your romantic beach getaway in mid-winter. Hopefully, from your own experience you'll know to book early and you wouldn't even think of asking for a discount—much the same as former servers always leave generous tips in restaurants!

Are You on the Right Side of the Law?

Don't forget there may be tax laws that you have to conform with, plus, your place should be in compliance with any safety regulations in your city, state and country. For example:

- If the apartment you are renting is on the second or third floor of the building, are you required to have two separate staircases or a fire escape?

- Do you need to have smoke detectors and carbon monoxide detectors installed?

- Is there a non-slip surface in the bathtub/shower?

- Are stairs obvious or do you need to create a visual cue letting people know there's a stair between rooms?

- Do you need to post exit instructions in case of a fire?

Some cities have to collect a "room" tax and you need to check this out before you start renting. In Mexico, this tax is 16 percent, in Europe, hosts must take a photo of the guests' passports and collect a city tax at the time of arrival.

You must also decide how and where you're going to pay income tax on the monies earned from your rental. If it is in the same country you live in, then you're probably going to treat it like a business, keep records of expenses and income and declare the funds when you file income tax. If the rental is outside of your home country, you may have a choice of where you pay the tax—in your home country or in the country in which the place is located. You need to consult a professional accountant to figure out what's the best scenario for you—and what best keeps you on the right side of the law.

Anecdote: Early in our renting experience we rented the place to a young couple who were friends of the family, for a low, low price. Under the verbal agreement, they were going to pay $400 for the house for one week, because they were driving from the States to our home and would be there only a week. It turned out their car was leased and you could not bring a leased vehicle into Mexico at that time (other countries have all kinds of intricate and weird rules, so you really have to check everything out).

They decided to fly and, since they were flying, they spent the entire two weeks of their vacation at the house—for the same $400. That $400 barely covered the costs of cleaning and laundry, plus, they broke a living room lamp that could not be replaced because I had brought it from the U.S. Communication is key, folks!

Earlier I mentioned the issue of including "quiet hours" in your house rules. This is becoming increasingly important as the home-sharing industry grows and rentals infiltrate traditional neighborhoods. You can get a lot of push-back from your neighbors if your guests are disturbing their peace. If you live in a resort area, most neighbors expect some partying and boisterous kids in swimming pools. If your unit(s) are located in a city or suburban neighborhood, this may not be acceptable to the people who actually live on your street.

This situation has happened with a house just a few blocks from ours in Buffalo. The house sleeps about a dozen people and has a large pool. It was purchased by a couple of private investors solely for the purpose of short-term rentals. The neighbors were tortured by loud pool parties all summer, and they did not respond kindly. A number of scathing emails were sent to the homeowners and more than once the police were called to the house.

You have three choices here: you screen renters and only accept parties that fit in with the neighborhood. State right in your description (AirBNB, for example, asks if you accept events) that your home "is not a party house" and don't book groups that are likely to get out of hand, such as wedding parties (sorry brides and grooms); you strictly enforce your noise rules (you have to be close by or have a diligent house manager); or you just let it slide and deal with angry neighbors like the Buffalo folks, who will probably end up sending you nasty letters and calling the police on your noisy guests.

If you intend to keep your business running for several years and you don't want more stress than necessary, I'd advise you to go with the first two options. For one thing, the more negative publicity generated around home-sharing, the more likely lawmakers, both local, state and federal, will look at the industry and think about regulating it. If your neighbors are suffering from disturbing noise your business could end up going away completely; and eventually, if enough push-back mounts up, the whole home-sharing business will follow suit.

Ensure You Have the Right Insurance

What does this mean? You have to be concerned that if someone is injured on your property or has their money or valuables stolen while they are staying at your place, they might consider suing you. Generally speaking, we live in a litigious society. People quickly look to the courts if they think they've been wronged.

Early in the renting game we had a group claim they had had $1,900 stolen out of the safe. There was no sign of forced entry into the house or the safe. We had told them *not* to leave a lot of money in the safe. We had no way of knowing what really happened at the house, and they didn't want to move out of it because they said they didn't feel it was unsafe to be there. Consequently, we did not offer to repay them (we had in our rental agreement that we would not give refunds for thefts), but we did offer them a free week at the house sometime in the future. Remember, they told us they did not feel unsafe in the house.

They wanted their money back, and tried to make a claim with our insurance company in the States. It was denied, that insurer did not cover our house in Mexico. We later took out an appropriate policy in Mexico, after we had the time to find the right company to handle our concerns.

Wherever you are renting, research insurance and make certain you have appropriate coverage for personal liability and theft. You may want to take out a large umbrella policy that covers multiple scenarios at a fairly reasonable cost.

Anecdote: The town we had our vacation home in evolved into party-city a few years after we built our house. People go there for destination weddings, family reunions and to surf. Naturally, things get out of hand once in awhile, so as good neighbors, sometimes we would just suck it up and let things slide (We thought that, as carefully as we tried to screen renters, we might be the house with the loud party at some time or another.). One of the times we didn't keep quiet, however, was when a particularly raucous wedding party was staying at the house across the street.

This house had a large, deep swimming pool and it just happened that an open, outdoor stairway leading to the second floor overhung the pool deck, coming within inches of overhanging the pool itself. I guess it was only a matter of time until someone thought it might be a good idea to climb over the railing and jump into the pool from the stairs — a dangerous prospect at the least, and even more dangerous when people had been imbibing in significant amounts of alcohol. This group elected to try out their daredevil act at four in the morning, after a wedding reception.

Needless to say, we were awakened from a sound sleep by the sound of laughter, music, and very loud splashes. Cal always kept one of those big bright flashlights (the kind you use for deer spotting) on hand for just such an occasion. He got out of bed, flashlight in hand, and illuminated the entire pool area across the street. That got their attention. The follow-up threat to call the police put a damper on the whole thing and the party soon came to an end. Next day we emailed the homeowners to tell them what had been going on (email was the only way to reach them), and I do believe they made an amendment to their house rules after that one. They would have been liable, had any serious injuries occurred, so it was worth mentioning "jumping from stairs into the pool" was prohibited.

Chapter 12

The Ins and Outs of Check-Ins and -Outs Are Not So Simple

Checking your guests in can be one of the trickiest parts of renting—both for you and the renters. Since there isn't typically a reception desk that's manned 24 hours a day, check-ins have to be coordinated around the time the renters expect to arrive. "Expect" is the operative word here. So much can happen to make renters late—planes are delayed, cars run into traffic jams, renters stop to shop—they can be late for any number of reasons.

Always ask for the renter's travel itinerary, so you can have an approximate time of arrival, and exchange cell phone numbers. Cell phones are not always reliable when they are used in a country that is not their home base, but they are better than nothing. Find out if the guests use "WhatsApp," or Skype which allows them to use their phone for texting and calling as long as it's attached to WiFi or the phone has cellular data. WhatsApp can be a lifesaver.

There are a number of ways to handle check-ins (none are infallible), so you may want to try more than one to find out what works best for you:

1. Wait at the house to meet the guests when they arrive. This works well if you are renting a room or a unit that's attached to your house, or even have an actual Bed and Breakfast. But, if you are not on site, you might end up spending quite a lot of your time sitting and waiting for people to arrive. You'll need

to be there well ahead of time, in case the guests arrive early.

2. If you or your house manager live within 10 or 15 minutes of the rental unit, have the guests call or text when they arrive. This can be a challenge in foreign countries, depending on if guests have an international plan or WhatsApp. If you're using WhatsApp, make sure you have the person in your contacts and vice versa before they leave for their trip.

3. Lockboxes or combination locks are the solution for some houses. This does simplify check-ins, because you can give your guests the combination before they arrive. The only problem with this is that you or your house manager won't get to meet the guests and go through the check-in instructions when they first arrive. If your house has some quirks that can be a problem. Houses can be a challenge to lock up, you may need to show people where things are, how appliances work, or where they should go for dinner or groceries. Meeting them gives you the opportunity to show them through the house and further set the tone for their visit.

If your place is in a rather obscure location, you can also set up a meeting at a public spot that is easy to find: a restaurant, gas station, or landmark. Meeting your renters (or having your house manager meet them) upon arrival helps establish a personal relationship with them. This will go a long way toward having them contact you if there's a problem, rather than waiting until they've gone home and then writing a negative review. On some web sites you get the opportunity to respond to the review, but proceed with caution. You don't want to look like you're taking the renter's remarks badly, and you don't want to get in a tinkling match with a skunk.

We had negative reviews where what our house manager and the renter said were completely contradictory so obviously, someone was not being truthful. Keep ALL email correspondence with renters and your staff so you have a way to check the information that has been exchanged. Then, if you have a rebuttal to something the renter has said, you have proof they were informed of the conditions before they booked. That way, you won't sound as though you're just angry about the poor review and expressing sour grapes.

Check-Outs

Check-outs tend to be a lot more relaxed than check-ins. Although you would think someone as obsessive-compulsive as I would want to scour the unit before the renters got into their cab, I never felt quite comfortable with that. Typically, either we, or the house manager, made a plan for the return of the keys, and if we happened to be there at the right time, we got to say goodbye. If not, we would have them leave the keys in a safe place, say goodbye early and call it a day.

We did go around and check things after people left, just to make sure nothing had been broken or was missing (or they had left something behind). Our house manager tended to leave that to the housecleaner, and that's not always practical. Some web sites return renters' damage deposits 24 hours after departure if the owner has not filed a complaint. It's nearly impossible to be sure the housecleaner goes through the house and reports to the house manager, who then reports to you within 24 hours.

I encouraged renters to tell me if something had been broken or damaged. Many of our furnishings came from the U.S., and if I wanted to replace them, I had to bring them from the U.S. again—they weren't available in Mexico. That was a good reason to ask the renters to let me know if anything got broken. We didn't charge people for small losses—that's part of the cost of doing business. We didn't have a lot of large losses. The largest was an area rug which we had to throw out thanks to a dog who needed Depends. By the time we knew about it, it was too late to file a claim with the web site. It wasn't a great expense because we got a deal on it (of course), but I do fondly remember driving from Buffalo to Sayulita in our Jeep with that rug between us for 3,600 miles because it just barely fit the full length of the interior of the car ...

Anecdote: Probably our worst check-in experience was the time we exchanged our house for a condo in Barcelona, and were seven hours late arriving because our flight was re-routed and delayed. The only way we had to communicate with the owner was by email—and our rendezvous location was a traffic circle near Torre de Mara, Spain—not the best arrangement! Our hosts ended up waiting the seven hours (part of them at the actual traffic circle) to meet us, giving us a tour of the condo and the town, and then facing a four-hour drive back to their home late at night. Fortunately they were warm, understanding people, and they had enjoyed their stay at our house, so they didn't seem to mind.

Just a few other memories: waiting five hours at the airport for guests arriving in Puerta Vallarta from

Quebec City, then driving the winding mountainous road to Sayulita at 2 a.m.; calling the owner of our B&B in Rome after a 12-hour day of traveling and getting no answer because she was in the basement; having guests wandering around Sayulita because I inadvertently sent them old directions for check in (a good reason to delete old files that have become obsolete).

Worst review experience: A group of nine people who came during the rainy season and voiced several complaints. Their taxi could not get up our hill so they complained they had to walk up, carrying their suitcases. Then they claimed they had been robbed, during the day, when a member of the party was at home, and the maid was there. Additionally, they complained about the "shacks with the tin roofs" down the street. First: they were told in an email it was the rainy season and at times the dirt road got washed out at that time of year (the organizer of the group said they were okay with that). Second: our house manager told us he had taken them and their suitcases up the hill in his truck, they did not walk. Third: there was no sign of forced entry, so we never established the true "facts" about the robbery. And fourth: they had been told, in an email and on the website, about the condition of the neighborhood on the street.

You can't win them all, but if you look at the big picture, the rewards of home-sharing rentals far outweigh the drawbacks.

Chapter 13

Bookkeeping 101

Your home-sharing business is just that: a business. Treat it as one, especially if you live in a high-cost area and are depending on it to help make your housing expenses. While you don't necessarily have to get a DOB/sole proprietorship or incorporate, you do need to keep as professional financial records as possible. You'll want to keep a "General Ledger (GL) spreadsheet" probably on a computer program such as QuickBooks, and you'll need to file all paperwork related to your rentals including receipts for expenses and payment records.

The home-sharing web sites provide regular statements as to how much they have paid out, however these can be tricky to locate on the sites. I've spent a fair amount of time on the phone with accounting people from the various sites finding out where the statements are—but they are available. If you collect money in some other way, through PayPal, actual checks from renters, etc., you will need to get statements from the other payment sites and keep a file of checks to prove how much you've earned. You'll want to put the amounts for every transaction into your GL spreadsheet, so you will know at the end of the year exactly how much you've collected.

Keep receipts or credit card statements showing what your expenditures were. These may include:

- Fees paid to list the unit on web sites.

- Labor and materials for improvements to the unit.

- All of those matching bedspreads, throw rugs and dishes you bought at the discount stores.

- Payments for services such as gas, electric and water.

- Payments to workers such as painters or housecleaners.

- Any travel expenses you incur going back and forth to your rental.

- Accountant, banking or consulting fees—even the cost of this book.

Definitely consult with an accountant to make sure you're keeping the right records. List all of your expenses in your GL spreadsheet, along with your income, so that at the end of the year you can figure out your profit (or loss). You will have to pay taxes on profit, so you want to be able to prove to the IRS or your country's federal tax agency exactly what the income and expenses were—just in case they decide to audit you.

You may be tempted to mingle your home-share money with your regular checking account, because if it's in a separate account you're going to end up doing a bit of transferring funds back and forth. It seems like a lot of extra trouble and expense to have a separate account for a small start-up business, but it's really worthwhile to keep the monies separate—after all, you could end up making more than you expect.

Epilogue

**Of course, there will be more sunsets in our future …
just not as many from this location, San Pancho,
Mexico.**

Since I began writing this book, we did sell the house in Mexico. It was getting to be too much maintenance for my husband and me, plus we wanted to have more time see a few other parts of the world while we are still healthy enough to travel. We are, however, continuing to rent through the home-sharing sites, and we might end up buying another property to rent out someday. The income was certainly worth the time and financial investment, as far as we were concerned.

We will miss the people we met through renting, since they almost always proved to be interesting. There was the couple who came to stay two months with their two small dogs, who used every surface (including the ironing board) in our small casita to put their copious amounts of stuff. Then we had Pete and Sue, who liked to come up for coffee in the mornings. Pete played guitar in a band at home in Minnesota and it didn't take him long to connect with a fellow in town who ran an open mike night in one of the local restaurants. Pete could also fix just about anything electrical and jumped in to do so whenever something was broken.

The "clothing optional" couple became good friends. Matt was an architect who liked puttering around houses and got a little bored on long vacations. Before long he was helping Cal with the "fix-it" chore list we always had going. By the end of the first week we didn't even think about whether they had clothes on or not—although Cal was a little surprised when he went down to the casita and found Jane happily cooking a meal, completely in the buff. Cal and Matt were such a great handyman team we invited him and Jane back the following November to help with the big pre-season clean-up/fix-up. Their company and help made power-washing, replacing lights, setting up shelving and refinishing window frames a lot more fun.

We had a young couple get engaged in the casita and a year later I officiated at their destination wedding. Most of the experiences were great, with the exception of a very few. Overall, we looked forward each year to meeting new people—and we're going to miss that.

In the meantime, we're excited about seeing new places, meeting new hosts, and learning new tips that (darn it), I could have put in this book had I thought of them …

Anecdote: Before I bring this book to a complete close, there's one more story—a story I've hesitated to include—you'll see why. One of our home exchanges was for a place in a warm, sunny, golf community (which will go unnamed). We were stopping there on our way home from Sayulita, so we had our cat with us. Our goal was to play golf every day for two weeks.

Cal had arranged the exchange and settled on dates with the homeowner about two months before we were to arrive. He was going to use our house at an unspecified time in the future, and told us he planned to leave his "sunny golf community" and return home just before we arrived. We had booked our plane tickets, he knew about the cat, and everything was all set—until two days before our arrival date. Cal got an email from "Jack," (not his real name) saying he had forgotten he had signed up for a golf tournament he just HAD to play in that weekend. Jack offered to pay for us to stay in a hotel for three nights, or we could come stay in the second bedroom of his home, but he and his girlfriend would be there for the three days.

We thought about the situation and since we had the cat with us, we elected to go to the house, rather than try to find a hotel that took cats and worry about what to do when the maid came to clean the room. It was only three nights. We were a little baffled as to the circumstances, but we always try to roll with the punches.

We rented a car at the airport and drove to the house, which was a lovely place located right on a golf course. Jack showed us our room and suggested we join him and his girlfriend for dinner at a local restaurant. The girlfriend was a little stand offish—apparently she was not fully on board with Jack's participation in the home-exchange business (but she didn't own the house so she didn't have much say). At the dinner, Jack explained the *golf tournament. It was a group of his friends from back home who got together every year to hold this event. They each put in a few dollars—well, more like one or two thousand—the grand prize was $30,000. They also bet significant amounts on each hole they played, I believe they call it "having skin in the game."*

It was instantly clear to us that Jack and his friends were in a slightly different league from us. As time progressed, Jack told us he had written a book on gambling and he gave us a copy to read. Then he invited Cal to play golf with him and two of his friends. Cal told him that when he and his friends put "skin in the game" it was $1 or maybe even $5 a hole, not the $1,000 a hole Jack's friends played for. Jack said that wasn't a problem, it was just a practice round. Cal had his game with Jack and the boys—and he learned that Jack played pretty good golf. He could play right-handed, left-handed and backwards. I am not exaggerating. It seemed Jack (well he did write the book on gambling after all) was pretty serious about winning.

As our luck would have it, Jack and the girlfriend stayed for the entire first week of our vacation, which was pretty uncomfortable since we didn't feel right about using the kitchen, plus they went to bed very early so we had to be quiet after eight o'clock. But we didn't want to offend them so we didn't say anything. We also didn't hear who won the "Nassau"—the big prize in the golf tournament. By that time we had figured out it wasn't a good idea to offend Jack or his friends. And I hope I'm not offending anyone by including this story because I don't swim well with cement overshoes …

Appendix 1

Letter to renters regarding protecting their money safe. This is specific to our locale; however, it can be adapted to a version relevant to your circumstances.

Recommendations for Handling Money in Mexico (or Any Foreign Country)

When Cal and I have visited European countries such as Italy, France and Spain, we have been warned to watch out for pickpockets—and if you follow Rick Steves at all, he writes about staying safe when you travel. My feelings are that we should talk to our guests about the issues that can occur in Mexico, which is why we're providing you with the following information.

Local police have made it clear to us that thefts are up all over Mexico, just as they are in other popular tourist destinations like the Bahamas and Jamaica. Thieves have become more professional and are able to get into any house and almost any safe. (You can use the safes if you want, we have put padlocks on them which have to be cut off, and therefore makes it more difficult for the thieves to open them. Combination safes have a high rate of failure.) Locally, it seems that criminals are almost exclusively interested in cash because it cannot be traced and is quick to grab. We don't hear of "breaking and entering" in Sayulita, however, we do hear of thefts that occur because someone got into a house. The most important safeguard is to lock the house when you leave, just as you likely do at your own home.

Disclaimer: We have done everything possible to make our house secure, however, as the police tell us, if someone wants to get into your house, they will. We are not responsible for any thefts at our house or casita. Over the years, however, we have developed the following strategies to avoid losses:

Before you leave home either purchase a prepaid credit/debit card for the amount of money you think you want to spend, or open a separate checking account (with a debit card) that you don't keep a lot of money in—say $500 as the maximum. If you have the checking account you can always transfer more money online if need be. With prepaid cards you can deposit additional funds into them if they run low.

Use ONLY those cards to get cash and then only use them at ATM machines that are indoors or—better still—at a bank or Mega. There is now an Intercam Bank in Sayulita and in town, the safest ATMs we have found are the one in the Chewbacca grocery store on Miramar and the one in Alas Blancas grocery store on Del Palmar in town. Several years ago our debit card was scammed and it was a group from the Ukraine, not Mexico!

Do not take out more cash at one time than you are comfortable losing (I realize this means more withdrawals and more ATM fees, but it will cost less in the long run than losing a large amount). Take your money and your valuables with you when you leave—or if you are going to keep them in the house, hide them and hide them well—not in the bedside table. Use the safe if you prefer, but make SURE you still lock up the ENTIRE house. The house manager should have shown you how to do this when you checked in, and there are also instructions in the renter's book, if you want to double-check.

ALWAYS lock up when you leave and at night!

Most thefts are crimes of opportunity—don't give the "*ladrones*" that opportunity.

Appendix 2

Letter to prospective renters regarding travel illnesses. Just as with the money article, you won't want to use this as-is, but you might want to adapt it to something suitable for your location.

Stay Healthy

Sayulita has become one of the top four towns in Mexico to be visited by tourists—but not all the news is positive. Much has been written online about visitors getting sick in Sayulita. We have a few recommendations that might help you avoid blowing one or two of your precious vacation days by getting sick.

Before you get on your plane, take Airborne or a similar product to boost your immune system.

Take hand sanitizer and sanitizing wipes on your trip, and wipe down your tray table, etc. We notice a lot of people get sick immediately after they arrive. It would be impossible for them to get these bugs in Sayulita, they must have come in contact with them on the plane.

Take probiotics before you arrive and during your stay. Yakult, is a yogurt-type of probiotic that's easy to take once a day to protect yourself, and if your stomach feels the least bit off, will help settle it.

Our maid is one of the best cleaners we have ever had in Sayulita, however, if we have a large turnover of guests, she may not have time to wipe down all door handles, etc. There are disinfectant wipes in the bathrooms and the back hall shelves. If you are one of those people who gets concerned about that type of thing, please use them to wipe down any surface you are worried about.

If someone in your party does get sick—once again, clean with the disinfectant wipes between maid cleanings so you aren't spreading anything through your group.

Do NOT eat at just any street stand—particularly the *"pasteur"* tacos. Look in our Renters Book for recommended restaurants. Do NOT take a chance on ceviche, fresh oysters on the beach, other beach food that has been in the sun all day.

During high season try to avoid swimming at the village center beach. It gets a lot of use and other areas, like Playa de los Muertos, Caractios, and the North Beach tend to have clearer water.

Appendix 3

Sample rental agreement. This was a generic agreement borrowed from another owner.

"Name or Address of House/Rental Unit" — Rental Agreement

Rental Policy

I understand my responsibilities as occupant and accept financial burden for any damages to the property caused by me or any member of my party. By signing below or *by making payment for my reservation*, I signify that I have read this agreement and accept the terms. I agree to pay the owners for repairs in the event damages are caused by us during our stay, and I agree to pay replacement value for any items which are broken during my stay. **The owners are not responsible for accidents or injuries to guests or for loss of money, jewelry or other valuables during their stay.**

We strongly advise you to keep only small amounts of cash and keep it with you at all times—or hide it—and hide it well, not in the bedside table. Do not put large sums of money in the safe as criminals know how to get into **all** safes—no matter what brand or type of lock. To ensure security, lock **all** gates and doors when you are gone and at night.

The owners are not responsible for any interruption in electrical service, as this may happen from time to time. While the owners make every effort to ensure that the guests' stay is enjoyable, the owners are not responsible for disturbances beyond their control including, but not limited to: town festivities, construction noise, early morning roosters and tropical storms, washouts of the road due to tropical storms -- or any other conditions of the road which are beyond the owners' control.

Payment

An initial deposit payment equal to 50% of the total in USD is required to make a reservation. The balance due, plus a credit card number as a security deposit, is due 15 days prior to arrival. In the event of a cancellation, the owners will attempt to re-rent the unit(s) for the reserved dates, in which case a full refund, minus a $50 USD administration fee, will be issued. Any dates not rented will be deducted from the initial payment and if no dates are rented, no refund will be issued.

Smoking

Smoking is not allowed anywhere inside the house.

Air Conditioning

In Sayulita, A/C is only necessary June through October. Since electricity is very expensive, it has to be used with caution. If you want to use the A/C in either the master bedroom or the casita, the house manager will give you the remote control, in exchange for an electricity surcharge of $30/week USD. You may pay him in pesos at the current exchange rate.

Noise

All guests agree to keep excessive noise to a minimum and be aware and respectful of the neighbors. If you are staying in the main house while the guest unit is occupied by someone else or vice versa, please be considerate of the other people's enjoyment. Loud noise or music is not permitted after 10 pm. Under no circumstances may any parties or events take place at the house. The owners take great care to make the house a relaxing place to enjoy while visiting, so to ensure the overall quality and appearance of the property these policies are strictly enforced.

Guests

The number of overnight guests (9 maximum for the house plus casita, 6 for the house alone, 3 for the casita) people allowed is the number of people stated on the reservation. Any increase must be approved prior to arrival and no more than the maximum occupancy for the property will be allowed. **If more guests than booked arrive, the house manager has the right to turn away the whole party without refunding the rental fee.** No guest may assign this agreement, sublet, or give permission for use of any part of the house to those not listed on the reservation -- including the pool.

Check-In

Check-in is at 2.00 pm, however the owners may be able to accommodate earlier arrivals. As soon as possible, please confirm with the owners your flight arrival and departure information and the time you would like to be met at the property Unless you notify us otherwise, the house manager or owners will be on time to let you in, show you the house, and give you keys.

Check-Out

Check-out is at 11:00 a.m. All keys should be returned to the house manager or the owners before leaving. Guests agree to pay $25 USD for each set of keys not returned (if a key is lost, this means we have to change the lock—not just replace the key). Inside the guest binder you will find an easy-to-follow list for checking out. Following these guidelines and leaving the house in the same condition as upon arrival will ensure there are no charges on your credit card for repairs or replacement of household furnishings. You will be notified in advance of any charges to be placed on your credit card regarding repairs or replacements.

Inspections

Owner or owner's agent will have the right to show the premises to prospective clients with 24 hour notice to Renter at Renter's convenience. The owner or owner's agent also has the right to inspect the premises at anytime if there is reasonable cause to believe the Renter or any other person is misusing or damaging the premises or furnishings therein.

Cancellation Policy

In the event of a cancellation, the owner will make every attempt to re-rent the unit(s) for dates reserved, in which case a refund will be issued minus any credit card processing fees and/or commissions incurred by owner (including any fees for processing the refund to a credit card), minus a $50 US administration fee. If any of the canceled days cannot be re-rented, the full booking amount for those days will be deducted from any refund due. If any canceled days are re-rented at a rate lower than what was paid for the canceled days, the difference will also be deducted from any refund due. The owner may consider a credit towards a future stay at his/her discretion. Any security deposit already paid will be fully refunded.

Acceptance of Terms

I declare I have read these provisions and that I accept and agree to the terms with full knowledge and

understanding of the consequences of any violation of the policies herein or of "Name or Address of House/Rental Unit." *Payment of the invoice for the deposit signifies acceptance of this policy.* (If so desired, sign, scan and email to: _____)

DATE: _____ GUEST SIGNATURE: _____

CPSIA information can be obtained
at www.ICGtesting.com
Printed in the USA
FFHW021624231019
55717757-61577FF